P9-BIF-944

Resolving Family
and
Other Conflicts

RESOLVING FAMILY AND OTHER CONFLICTS

EVERYBODY WINS

by Mendel Lieberman
& Marion Hardie

Copyright © *1981 by Mendel Lieberman and Marion Hardie*

ALL RIGHTS RESERVED

Published by Cymbidium Books

Formerly Published by ORENDA/Unity Press

SECOND EDITION — 1984

Lieberman, Mendel H.   1913-
   Resolving family (& other) conflicts so that everybody wins.
   Bibliography: p.
   Includes index.
   1. Marriage counseling—United States.   2. Communication
in marriage.   I. Hardie, Marion, 1929-
joint author.   II. Title.
HQ10.L48   306.8'7   80-25270
ISBN 0-913300-52-7
ISBN 0-913300-50-0 (pbk.)

Additional copies can be purchased by enclosing $10.00, postpaid,
to: Cymbidium Books, 13393 Sousa Lane, Saratoga, CA 95070.

Printed in the United States of America

   3 5 7 9 8 6 4 2

To Barbara McCain and all those other students, clients, family members, and friends with whom we learned and continue to learn.

Contents

PART FOUR

PARTICULAR PROBLEMS

PART FIVE

THE EVER-RENEWING RELATIONSHIP

Resolving Family
and
Other Conflicts

A Word From Mendel

THERE IS A LOT OF PAIN in families (and in other human systems) that doesn't have to be there. There is a lot of hope, aliveness, and joy ready to flower when family members and members of other human systems can learn how to nourish these positive qualities.

My twin convictions about pain and hope grow stronger with each day that I work with individuals, couples, families, groups, and work teams. Whether they seek me out as "therapist," "counselor," or "consultant," or whatever term they use, they all seem to be saying, each in his or her own way, "I hurt; please help me."

At the other end, when the course of sessions is completed and successful, there is great variety in how people express the outcome. Some simply say, "Wow!" Some say, "I really did it myself, didn't I?" Some say, "Sometimes I wonder why I stayed stuck so long," or "I had forgotten that there could be such caring in our relationship"; and some say, "Our productivity is up 12 per cent."

This is not to say that all marriages can be "saved" or that all relationships can be made harmonious. In some, the success that crowns the effort is the choice to terminate the relationship. And not all courses of therapy or counseling are crowned by even that much success; sometimes the parties terminate their efforts before attaining any measure of conscious satisfaction. So I make you no promises.

You may find, however, that your experience will match mine: the methods presented in this book may suggest options that you had not seen before. These options may increase your sense of power in the world. And they just might increase your actual power to get more viable, rewarding, enriching relationships.

I have intended the words in this book to be a very personal word from me to you. In writing, I found myself many times falling back into the custom that authors have of making their advice sound authoritative. If you come across any parts of the book that seem to say, "This is The Truth; you should accept it because I am an authority," I hope you will let me know, so that I can revise it. What I want to do is share my experience with you. My "truth" is based not on The Truth (which is not known to me) but on my experience, known through the filter of how accurately I can perceive it, how completely I can recall it, and what sense I am able to make of it.

I have seen in counseling that the experience of one person *can* be communicated to and shared with another. The experience is transformed in passing from the Sender to the Receiver, but the Receiver can use both the experience transmitted and the experience of the transmittal to alter his or her own experience and perceptions, heighten his or her self-esteem, get in touch with power never before tapped, and create life-enhancing solutions.

It was so important to me to be open and personal in addressing these words to you that I felt some discomfort at using the words "we" and "us" in early drafts of the manuscript. "We" and "us" would have been accurate, because Marion and I are co-authors, and have tried to give you the product not only of my experience but of hers as well. But every time I saw "we" or "us" in the manuscript, it sounded like the "editorial we" that newspapers and magazines often use as a form of anonymity.

Marion solved the problem. "You are doing the basic writing," she said. "So make it yours: your words, your style, how you see the world, and how you express and realize yourself in it. My contribution will be to go over what you have written, and take responsibility for making it reflect me in the first person singular as fully as you have made it reflect you in the first person singular."

"Not just an editorial job," I said. "That wouldn't do you justice."

She laughed. "One thing you know about me is that I am my own spokesperson, and I do not take a submissive back seat. I get a lot of support from you in that."

"More than support. Encouragement. Delight."

"And you have my support," she said, "in doing the writing—in the first person singular. I'll take responsibility for making the final draft represent my views as well as yours. And if we disagree—well, we know how to fight that out to a loving conclusion."

And we do. And we did.

PART ONE

Winners and Losers

1

Getting to be a Winner

TAPED TO THE WALL in front of my desk is this note: "It works. Alan."

Alan was one of the doubters. He came to one of the earliest classes Marion and I offered on the subject of "Resolving Family Conflicts so that Everybody Wins." He scoffed. The gospel according to St. Alan was that somebody had to win and somebody had to lose, and he was damned if he was going to lose.

It became apparent before the first class session was an hour old that Alan was a consistent loser. His marriage was a wreck (her fault). His job gave him no satisfaction (the boss's fault). With his children he experienced no pleasure (their fault).

When we presented active listening and six-step problem solving, Alan's lip curled. It sounded phony. It would never work.

Our class consists of ten weekly sessions, three hours each. Alan's note came after the third session.

We have grown accustomed to transformations and testimonials like Alan's. We have seen long-standing parent-child conflicts lose their sting, failing marriages take on new life, dysfunctional office staffs increase productivity and profit, screaming and hitting in families give way to caring and joy.

What makes the difference? I think the basic ingredients are these:

1. I feel good about myself (self-esteem).
2. My partner feels good about himself or herself.
3. My partner and I communicate in ways that enhance and strengthen each other's self-esteem.

That's all? I think so. Let's see.

From Win-Lose to Win-Win

If I make you wrong, I lose. I don't want to lose. I deserve better than that; I deserve to win. To win, I have to make you right. I can make you right without making myself wrong. I can make you right without losing. I can make you right and make myself right at the same time. That way we both win. That is the only way for me to win. The only way for me to win is to make sure we both win. If one of us loses, we both lose.

Does that sound like a riddle? It's not. It is what I consider to be the first principle in human relationships. Why does it sound so confusing? The no-lose principle is not difficult or confusing in itself, but most of us have been brought up and trained in methods of making others wrong. The result is that human relationships, with few exceptions, are a mess. And the people who grow up in those relationships suffer from such low self-esteem that a whole profession (psychotherapy and related fields) has grown up just to help them find out they are really OK.

This book is about how people in human relationships can win—can, in fact, be winners—and how, in the process, they can make their relationships successful, joyful, stimulating, confirming, rewarding, fulfilling, alive, peaceful, restful, actualizing. And they can open up for themselves, and the others in their relationships, the realization of their essential rightness, goodness, beauty, and full potential.

How?

Let me start again with that first principle, reversing it this time, because it is as valid from you to me as it is from me to you.

If you make me wrong, you lose. You deserve better than to lose; you deserve to win. To win you have to find a way to make me right. You can make me right without making yourself wrong. You can make me right without losing. You can make me right and make yourself right at the same time. That way we both win. That is the *only* way for you to win. The only way for you to win is to make sure we both win. If one of us loses, we both lose.

That is what this book is all about.

No-Lose Solutions

Imagine a husband and wife, one of whom votes Republican and the other Democratic. They argue and argue with increasing heat and frustration, and possibly with more and more rancor, but to no avail. Their basic messages are likely to be, "You are wrong and I am right. I blame you."

How, then, are they to arrive at a solution in which both may feel like winners? The answer lies in separating *content* from *process*. *Content* is *what* the parties are talking about; *process* is *how* they are discussing that content in the context of their relationship. Presumably the relationship is of value to both partners; and it is this value which gives the disagreement over content its emotional charge. Valuing that relationship, the partners have an interest in not damaging it, or each other, in stating their respective positions. More than that, they can voice the concern and respect that each feels for the other, and can make room in the relationship to allow the value differences between them to continue to exist. The basic position of each is, "Given the background of my experience, I make sense and order out of my world in one way. Given the background of your experience, you make sense and order out of your world in another way. My way is valid for me; your way appears to be valid for you. That is one of the differences between us in a relationship in which each of us cherishes the other and validates the other's way of being in the world."

But what do you do when some behavior of mine is a problem to you, particularly if it is odious, offensive, thoughtless, or even deliberately hurtful? At such times it is hard for you not to make me wrong. Your resentment and indignation are likely to move you to shoot angry words and blames at me like bullets. You will probably *want* to make me wrong, to wring an acknowledgement from me that I *was* wrong, perhaps to get an apology from me, and even to withhold your forgiveness as a way of punishing me a little further.

These attitudes and responses are almost automatic with many people, including, sometimes, myself. I am not saying, "Don't do these things"; I am saying only that they don't work. They don't produce any results that feel good. They damage the relationship. They reduce, or may reduce, the other person's self-esteem, and they produce defensiveness, resistance, resentment, and antagonism, which increase the likelihood that the offending party will repeat the objectionable behavior or invent new ones.

So what are you to do when my behavior is objectionable to you? For those occasions, Part Three of this book presents an array of problem-solving and conflict-resolving techniques and skills. I have found them to be effective not only in stopping or modifying the objectionable behavior, but also, at the same time, in strengthening the relationship and enhancing the self-esteem of its members.

Self-Esteem

High self-esteem is the bedrock for forming and maintaining successful and nurturing relationships. The person with high self-esteem is less defensive, and consequently more open to the other members wants and feelings. The person with high self-esteem is less needy and is more free in his or her relationships to give love and approval as free gifts, rather than as the purchase price for maintaining a relationship based on need and fear. The person with high self-esteem is less likely to distort or to misperceive the transactions within the relationship because of remembered experiences, and is more likely to be in the real transaction of the moment. So the success of the relationship depends largely on the self-esteem that its members bring to the relationship or acquire during its life.

The reverse is also true: the self-esteem of the members of a relationship is substantially affected by how they experience the relationship. If they feel nurtured, validated, affirmed, accepted, and supportively included by the other member or members, their self-esteem is strengthened.

So the process is circular: individuals with high self-esteem bring with them the capacity to form and maintain successful, nurturing relationships; and nurturing relationships, in turn, elevate and enhance the self-esteem of their individual members. Whatever is done by participants in an intimate relationship to support, sustain, and enhance the self-esteem of other participants contributes to making that relationship successful, alive, and growthful. Whatever has the effect of injuring, impairing, or diminishing the self-esteem of other participants is hurtful and injurious to the relationship, and by that fact constitutes a loss to the participant producing the injury.

Let's take a three-fold look at self esteem in your intimate relationships:

1. What affects self-esteem?
2. How can you enhance your own self-esteem?
3. How can you enhance the self-esteem of your partners in this relationship?

First, what affects self-esteem? I find it useful to think of self-esteem as consisting of five parts, related as shown in Figure 1.1: (a) a sense of physical integrity, which is the foundation of all the other parts; (b) the

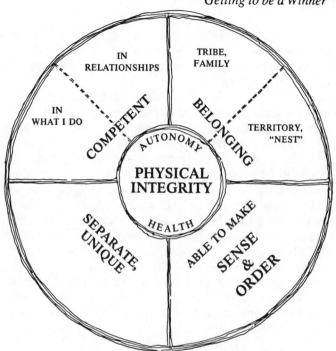

SELF-ESTEEM MODEL

Fig. 1.1

feeling of being able to make sense and order out of the world; (c) a sense of competence; (d) a feeling of belonging; and (e) a perception of separateness and uniqueness.

Physical Integrity

Physical self-acceptance seems to underlie the other four aspects of self-esteem. Feeling good about our own bodies needs to be established as early as possible. Frederick LeBoyer, the French obstetrician, has suggested a method, which has gained wide acceptance, of making the birth process more human and loving than it has been. Rather than in brightly lit, clinical operating rooms, deliveries are made in dimmer light. Instead of being held upside-down, struck on the behind, and whisked off by a nurse, the infant is laid across the mother's belly, to be gently fondled and awakened while the umbilicus is severed. This procedure is based on the premise that the new, little person has an integrity of rightness that we can discover by paying attention to its ways of expressing itself by crying, sucking, startling, etc. It is also premised that if we respect this integrity, the child will feel more secure, more self-confident, more self-reliant, more capable of giving and getting love and respect.

A similar view is reflected in self-demand feeding. The theory is that babies know when they are hungry and when they are not, and that, by feeding them according to their own rhythms, we reinforce their sense of their own rightness and worthwhileness.

Toilet training is another opportunity for reinforcing the child's sense of autonomy and physical integrity. In the child's mind, its eliminative functions are its "own." Some children are emphatically assertive about this. They have control over when and where and how often to urinate and move their bowels, and they seem stubbornly determined not to relinquish this power. (A little person does not have much power, after all.) Too many parents make a power struggle out of this situation, with the result that the child may learn to capitulate and placate and be a loser, or to maintain an attitude of wariness, distrust, and hostility, possibly throughout life. Instead, toilet-training time can be the occasion for reinforcing the child's sense of physical integrity and for enhancing self-esteem. (We will take a look at how to do this in Chapter 9.)

There are many other ways in which autonomy and physical integrity are violated, with negative effects on self-esteem. One of these is picking up and carrying a child to where he or she is resisting going. Another is excessive tickling. Still another is corporal punishment. Rape is another. And children may experience an enema as a similar violation.

Another part of the consciousness of physical integrity is a feeling of health or wholeness. Chronically ill health is often seen to diminish self-esteem. Many women who have suffered surgical removal of a breast seem to feel much less self-worth. Even malfunctions or surgical removal of parts that don't show appear sometimes to be experienced as degrading. And the debilitating effects of advancing age may be seen to reduce self-esteem among some older people.

How can we enhance our own self-esteem in terms of our physical integrity? For me, the one most important discovery in this area was that I had a right to ask for what I wanted. I had a right to draw attention to myself to gratify my physical needs and wants, not only as an infant, but also as an adult. A related right was that my partner had a right to say NO (see p. 22). Another right was the right to acceptance by other members of my family (club, camp, etc.) and the right (indeed, the necessity) to accept myself just as I am. For example, I was afraid of the water. I could get some help from family and friends in my attempts to overcome the fear, but I needed something more. I needed family and friends to help me accept the fear if I so desired.

Making Sense and Order of the World

I have had the experience of doubting my own sanity. For me, it is a very scary experience. I have discovered with much help from others that the answer is to be found in my own body feelings. I have to remind myself as I remind my clients and intimate members of my family and others close to me to trust my body. Yes, I am aware that my body can betray me, because it is loaded with old prejudices and biases, misperceptions and misconceptions. But I have never found its equal. Trust your body. Then go to work testing the reliability of the information that is stored away in your intuition. And let your partner have the experience of your encouraging him or her to trust his or her body messages.

Making sense and order out of my world is a never-ending process, beginning with the first awakening of consciousness. As an infant I learn to associate my hunger with the noise I make in crying, and to associate my crying with the satisfaction of that hunger. That association contributes to my sense of being in an orderly and predictable world. As I grow and learn, I translate those associations into expectations, and I learn that subsequent events do or do not confirm my expectations. If subsequent events do confirm my expectations, my feeling of being able to make sense and order out of my world is strengthened. If events do not confirm my expectations, I must go through the anxiety of being unable to predict and of reviewing my associations and revising my expectations.

The more I can make my world predictable, or at least comprehensible, the more I can regard myself as basically OK (see Appendix A, item 2). The more I regard myself as OK and the safer my world seems to me, the more free I am to be outgoing and accepting toward others, and the less need I have to be defensive or rigid.

The process of making sense and order out of one's world goes on throughout life. But people vary widely in their ability to handle situations of which they cannot easily make sense or order. Moreover, each individual shows varying capacities for handling such situations at different times of his or her life. An infant, with very little experience to draw on, may very well translate a confusing or crazy-making experience into "I am crazy." A mature adult with high self-esteem, on the other hand, may suffer little or no self-doubt in a crazy-making situation.

Members of intimate systems (such as families) stand to profit from examining their behaviors to see whether they contribute to or detract from the sense that other family members have of being able to make order out of or find meaning in their worlds.

Feeling Competent

Janna, age three and a half, was very proud. She had put on her own shoes after her nap, all by herself.

"See, Mommy," she announced proudly, looking down at her feet.

Mother responded critically, "You have them on the wrong feet."

Not to be defeated, Janna responded logically, "They're the only feet I have."

Building the sense of competence is another process that continues throughout life. The sense of competence seems to have two parts. One part is competence in what I do. We see small children learning to grasp and hold a spoon, learning to lift food to their mouths, learning to walk more surely and fall down less, learning not to move their bowels until they get to the bathroom, and a host of other muscular and physical attainments. Manual and physical skills enhance self-esteem, as does a sense of competence in earning money, performing an occupation, meeting emergencies, and the like.

The second part of the sense of competence is competence in relationships. When the child learns to grasp a spoon, there may be a feeling of achievement. If the mastery of that skill is greeted with sounds of delight and approval from the grownups in the child's life, the child experiences a kind of competence in social relationships that is vital to the child's self-esteem. The ability to evoke expressions of approval and acceptance from the parent figures in the child's life will be tested over and over again. Later this testing will extend beyond the immediate family. Competence in human relationships with teachers and fellow students will be tested. The dating rituals of teenagers are ways of testing social competence, as are some of the battles in which siblings engage. And when each individual forms her or his own family, a sense of being competent or incompetent in those relationships will be crucial to the individual's self-esteem and to the success of the relationship. This is one reason why divorce is felt by many persons to be intolerable; it is experienced as a failure, signifying incompetence in the relationship, and thus a blow to self-esteem.

One way to enhance feelings of competence is to be a model of acceptant behavior; another is to risk experiencing competence, either actually or in fantasy or trance.

Belonging

The third quadrant of self-esteem is the sense of belonging, of having a secure place or "home." This belonging is in two parts. One part consists of the family or tribe of which the individual considers herself or himself to be a member. This part of the sense of belonging is more than just a place at the table or in the tribal councils—although that sense of place is important, too. The individual's place in the relationship must be such that the individual knows without question that she or he makes a difference, that his or her absence or presence matters to the other members, and that the individual is automatically included among "us" in any formulation of "us and them."

The second aspect of belonging has a kind of nesting or territorial quality. Children who are moved often from town to town or school to school seem to need a more predictable place with which to identify. Conversely, being able to furnish a home or apartment to reflect its occupants seems to elevate their self-esteem.

Feeling Separate, Unique

Separated by only a fine line from physical autonomy, is the sense of being separate and unique. My self-esteem requires that I feel myself to be one of a kind and special, and that I be able to accept my specialness comfortably, even gladly. I learn that attitude from observing that the significant others in my life accept my uniqueness and encourage me to optimize it. They do that by letting me know there is room in the relationship for me to be different in my values and perceptions, that my feelings, like my size, shape, and color, are all right because they are mine. They encourage me to learn at my own pace. They support me in listening to my body's messages about when I am tired, hungry, afraid, anxious, or whatever. In exercising my separateness, I do not jeopardize my place in my family or tribe. I have my place in the nest. That place is securely mine. And I can make it reflect my uniqueness.

Building Self-Esteem

When the self-esteem of any family member is low, it is in the interest of all members to be concerned. Briefly, the task is for all members to provide an environment in which healthy people grow with children. The parent or parents or parent figures treat them with respect. They touch the youngsters in affectionate ways, and welcome the touchings that come back to them. They support and reinforce the child's exercise of choice rather than passing judgments on the decisions made.

For adults, the treatment is approximately the same. We let them know of our love and acceptance.

Dorothy Corkille Briggs presents a seven-point formula for enhancing the self-esteem of children. I offer here a similar formula in my own words, modified by my own thoughts, applicable to all members of intimate relationships, children and adults. I want to suggest some ways for strengthening and increasing the self-esteem of all members of relationships.

1. Genuine encounter. To feel loved, every individual needs focused attention, communicating genuine interest. This does not mean self-sacrifice, on the one hand, or excessive expectations, on the other. It means taking the time necessary to communicate fully your genuine interest in the other.

If my partner says, "I am afraid of that interview tomorrow," I don't try to talk him or her out of feeling afraid. I reflect back the fear I'm hearing. And by my concerned attention, I validate my partner's importance in the world. Or if my four-year-old son shows me a picture he has drawn, I reflect back the importance that he attaches to it rather than centering on the quality or reality of the product.

If I sense in myself a lowering of self-esteem, I can ask for my partner's attention. I may have to ask for it more than once, but I can usually get it if I am assertive enough. Or I can turn to another family member, share my need, and make a request.

2. The safety of trust. The basic ingredients in building trust in oneself and the capacity to trust others are openness and congruence. To experience trust in a relationship, your partner or partners need to experience your humanness and your genuineness. They need to know your feelings, your reservations, and your ambivalences. They need to see that your body language matches your words. And they need to be able to count on you to be for yourself, to care about them, to be clear in communicating, and to be as consistent as you can be within the limits of your right to change. They learn to trust themselves by experiencing your trust in them, your trust that they can handle their own feelings, develop competence and judgment, and exercise their autonomy responsibly.

3. The safety of nonjudgment. A member of an intimate relationship thrives best when he or she is accepted without judgment. This means without affirmative judgments as well as without negative judgments. I have noticed a number of times that the children of happy, functional families ordinarily exhibit much more creativity, innovation, and variety in their art work and in their fantasies than do the children of most dysfunctional families. The difference seems to be that parents in dysfunctional families tend to judge the products of their children's creativity in terms of good, bad, pretty, nice, ugly, etc., whereas the parents in more functional families tend to pay more attention to the child's own thoughts, feelings, purposes, and growth in engaging in creative pursuits. (See the discussion on approval or disapproval as a communication stopper in Chapter 5.) Examples of judgmental comments are: "You're playing your scales a lot better than you used to," and "Your handwriting has improved a lot." Examples of nonjudgmental comments are: "You seem to feel more confident in playing your scales," and "I'm guessing that you feel pretty good about your handwriting now."

4. The safety of being cherished. Each individual in a relationship needs to have his or her specialness or uniqueness acceptantly recognized, and to feel that his or her place in the relationship is secure and is not conditional. It may feel good to be told I have a lovely body, but if I take that message to mean that I am loved *because* my body is lovely or *as long as* my body is lovely, the underpinning of my self-esteem is shaky. With the feeling of being cherished comes the readiness to seek more realistic goals, to accept others as they are, to learn more efficiently, to be more creative, and to like myself.

Marj sometimes had trouble liking herself. Her solution was imaginative. Mentally she "created" a new, loving mother, perfect for her in every way. This mother image cherished her with no conditions or exceptions, and was available to her at all hours of the day and night.

5. The safety of "owning" feelings. It is important to me to own the feelings that I express to you. For example, if I am envious of your success or jealous of the attention paid to you by someone else and not paid to me, it is important to me to own these feelings as mine and not to resort to the fiction that "you made me" envious or jealous or that you are not worthy of my trust. I want to be particularly careful not to blame you. Furthermore, I want you to acknowledge the natural rightness of my having whatever feelings (and hair color and body type) I have, and I want to let you own your feelings without withdrawing my approval or acceptance of you as a person valued in our relationship. If you express fear or anger, for example, I do not want you not to be afraid or angry. I want to hear your feeling as valid for you when you are feeling it, and I want to respect your power and ability to handle your feeling according to the way you have learned to make sense and order out of your world. I want to do this without withdrawing from you, and without intruding on you, and certainly without judging you. If our feelings about things differ, I want to make room in the relationship for that difference to exist with mutual respect. ("Owning" feelings is discussed in Chapter 2.)

6. The safety of empathy. When I am most able to feel empathy for another person, I have an almost physical sense—amounting to more than understanding—of what it's like to be the other person in that moment. This is not the same as sympathy. When I feel sympathy, it is a compassionate concern for the other person's situation. When I feel empathy, it is more like being in and experiencing the other person's being in a situation. If my own self-esteem is low, my ability to empathize will be small. Similarly, I will not be able to empathize very well if I do not genuinely feel caring for the other person. When I am able to empathize, I am aware of its great power to nurture the other person and to diminish alienation. When another person in your relationship is upset, the need is usually not for understanding or advice or help or factual clarification (see Communication Stoppers, Chapter 5), but for your empathic support and acceptance, as evidenced, for instance, by active listening (see Chapters 4 to 6).

7. The safety of unique growing. Each person needs the freedom to grow in his or her own direction at his or her own pace. Growth includes plateaus and even regressions. Freedom to grow is limited if it is not accompanied by freedom to retreat. In TA terms (see Appendix A), the internal Child, when pressured to grow or change, is likely to dig in its heels rebelliously and to refuse. Growth comes when nurturing parenting, from outside or within the individual, okays the internal Child just as it is.

Patti came home from kindergarten, and I noticed a dark frown instead of her usual smile.

"How was school today?" I queried.

"Okay," without much enthusiasm.

"You look troubled. Are you feeling frowny?" I persisted.

"Michael doesn't like me," she answered; a pause, and then, "what d'you s'pose is wrong with him?"

But What About Me?

The various ways of enhancing the self-esteem of other family members applies equally to you. The win-win principle includes your winning along with other family members. Indeed, for your children (partners, employees, etc.) to develop a healthy sense of being able to make meaning and order out of their world, they need to know that no-lose means no-lose for you as well as for them. They need to know that they can count on you to be for yourself as well as for them. At the same time that they are learning they can count on you to mean what they say, they need to learn also that you have a right sometimes to change your mind. For them to develop a sense of competence, they need the security of knowing that you will take responsibility for standing up for your rights in the relationship, and not leave that responsibility to them at a time in their lives when their judgment, experience, and physical and emotional properties are not strong enough that they can reliably tell sound from unsound limits.

Here are some rights that parents sometimes fail to exercise. Each right is connected with a responsibility.

1. The right to place firm limits on the behavior of their children that would otherwise infringe on the rights of other people (including the parents). The responsibility is to teach the child the limits of socially acceptable behavior and the gratification that accompanies social competence.

2. The right to stand your ground and follow through with discipline when the child tests the limits. The responsibility is to teach the child that consequences are unavoidable when they transgress the rights of others.

3. The right to require responsible work as participants in the meaningful work of the household. The responsibility is to teach the child the gratification of sharing and enjoying work. Good work is part of good living.

4. The right to take time off from the job of being a parent. The responsibility is to teach the child that our work and our children do not possess us and that our physical presence is not necessary for the child's survival.

5. The right to be truthful about your feelings, ideas, thoughts, and values. The responsibility is to model openness, genuineness, awareness, and two-way communication.

There are some pseudo-rights that parents sometimes mistakenly think they have.

1. The right to know everything their children think. Children have the right to the privacy of their thoughts.

2. The right to their children's approval and understanding. Children may not always understand or approve of their parents, and they have the right to complain or disagree.

3. The right to tease or laugh at their children. Even when these practices take place "in fun," they undermine self-esteem and may kindle destructive rage in the victim.

4. The right to expect love. This is theirs to give or to withhold.

5. The right to expect respect. Respect is a privilege earned and deserved by parents who exercise their legitimate rights and discharge their responsibilities as parents and as caring human beings.

2

Feelings and the You
in the Relationship

BEING AWARE OF FEELINGS and being able to express them appropriately are the keys to effective use of the methods described in the
following chapters. Before we examine the methods themselves, let's
make sure we know how to work the keys.

Suppose you would like to go to the mountains for a vacation with
your partner, but your partner prefers to go to the seashore. You each
feel very strongly about your preference. How is the impasse to be
resolved? In some situations, families manage to resolve these conflicts
without going into feelings. They may resort to persuasion. They may
bring books and pamphlets and other kinds of factual information to
bear on the dispute. They may resort to threats or commands or other
forms of coercion. They may compromise, *e.g.*, decide to go to the
desert instead of either the mountains or the seashore.

In my experience, however, the families that seem most successful as
families, and most nurturing to their individual members, tend to
resolve these conflicts not so much in terms of *content* (what the conflict
is about) as in terms of *process* (how the family members feel about one
another and about the relationship as they go through the process of
working out a solution to the conflict). This type of resolution is most
effectively carried out when all parties to the dispute are aware of their
own feelings, are open and congruent in expressing their feelings, and

are aware of and concerned about the feelings of the other parties to the dispute. Members of these families generally feel good about themselves, comfortably use many words expressing feelings, particularly in their significant relationships, and are comparatively assertive in saying what they want.

The reverse is also true. People with low self-esteem appear to be far less aware of their feelings, express their feelings less often, use far fewer words expressive of feelings, and are comparatively less assertive and clear in expressing what they want. They also appear to be less sensitive to and less considerate of the feelings, wants, and needs of others, except that they appear to be relatively afraid and reluctant to say "no" directly and clearly to the expressed wants of others.

What Are Feelings?

The word "feelings" is used in a confusing variety of ways. For instance, I often hear people say, "I feel that you are not listening to me," or "I have the feeling that you are hostile to me right now." These are not feelings; these are, at the most, perceptions. In fact, they may be no more than assumptions, suppositions, or guesses. Whenever you hear somebody say, "I feel *that*...," you can be pretty sure that the words which follow will express not a feeling but, more likely, a perception, opinion, or conclusion of some sort.

Similarly, feelings are not the same as judgments. "I feel that what you did was wrong" is not a feeling; it is the expression of a judgment. Another expression of a judgment is, "I don't feel that this product is worth the price."

So what are feelings? In this book, I use the word to mean principally a set of emotions and other bodily reactions and responses, like those appearing in Appendix C. I offer many words there to try to counteract the poverty of feeling words displayed by many individuals in our culture; but the list is not exhaustive.

Expressing Feelings: An Investment of the Essential Person

More than any other quality, feelings define the essence of a person, and the expression of feelings is an investment in the relationship.

In my perception, a person is not known unless and until that person's feelings are known. I have worked with couples who have been married fifty or more years. They come to me in pain. Their relationships are not going well, and their marriages are in question. They look to me to help them break out of their pain. In many of these troubled marriages, I find that one or both partners are not fully aware of their own feelings or of their partner's feelings, and are not accustomed to including the language of feelings in their communications with one another. When I ask one partner what the other partner is probably feeling about a situation that arises during the counseling hour, I find that they do not know each other (after all those years!) well enough to be able to guess fairly accurately how the other partner feels in the painful situations under discussion. Conversely, when these couples have become more aware of feelings generally, and of their own feelings in particular, and have become more comfortable and adept at expressing feelings in their daily communications, the sense of intimacy flowers, and conflicts come to be resolved in a more healing manner.

It is as if a person is not fully a person without feelings, and must feel incomplete when awareness of feelings is blocked. Similarly, one's partner is not known and cannot be fully loved or cherished if his or her feelings are not known.

I am not saying that a person is fully defined by feelings alone. Your thoughts are also part of your essence. What you do is part of your essence. Indeed, each person is so multifaceted and unique that he or she is beyond definition. Who are you? You are that you are. No definition is adequate.

In your relationships, however, you are neither defined nor known unless your partner (or partners) in the relationship knows your feelings as openly and completely as you can possibly make them known. Moreover, in making your feelings known, you render yourself vulnerable to rejection and hurt. The revelation of your feelings is a risk. And your electing to take that risk is an expression of trust and an investment in the relationship.

Congruent expression of feelings is an investment of another kind. It constitutes an encouragement and a model for others in the relationship to recognize and trust their own feelings and processes, and so helps them to have access to more essential information in their lives and their relationships.

Your congruent expression of your feelings also helps other members of your relationships toward sanity. I remember a mother and her twelve-year-old son who came to me for help in learning to communicate with each other. At one point the mother burst into tears. The son looked up and said, "Are you crying?" The mother replied, "No." This is what I call a crazy-maker. Her tears were plain to see, but her words instructed her son not to trust the evidence of his senses. My experience of children is that they are keenly sensitive and intuitive in picking up feelings and emotions in their parents. If their parents are open in showing and expressing their feelings and emotions, the children learn to trust their own perceptions and intuitions. If, on the other hand, the parents are not congruent and open in expressing feelings and emotions, the children learn to distrust their own perceptions and intuitions, or the truth of their parents' statements, or both. To some children these contradictions in parental messages are intolerably confusing; so these children find refuge by shutting themselves off from what most of us call reality.

In the chapters that follow, I therefore emphasize the value of straight, direct, open, honest, congruent expression of feelings, wants, needs, and emotions, so that communications may be clear and effective, and so that relationships may be nurturing and the individuals in them self-actualizing.

Unawareness of feelings and a poverty of words to express feelings go hand-in-hand with what many persons describe as an emptiness, an absence of a sense of who they are. I no longer find it remarkable that, as these individuals progress in counseling or therapy, the growth of their confidence and of their sense of completeness, self, and identity coincide with an increasing awareness of their internal processes, including feelings, and with growth of their ability to describe and to define these processes and feelings.

The culture in which many of us grew up teaches us in many ways not to have the feelings we have, not to express the feelings we have, not to let it be known that we have the feelings we have, to keep a firm grip on our emotions, to suppress many of them if we can, and to regard feelings as somehow unnatural, undesirable, shameful, unreal, and having no independent validity.

One way in which we are subtly taught to discount feelings is by direct injunction: "Don't cry, dear," or "Cheer up," or "Keep smiling," or "Now pull yourself together," or "Be brave."

Sometimes the command is in the form of a comparison with some ideal, such as, "Boys don't cry," or "Anger doesn't do any good," or "Now, be a big girl," or "Look at Daddy; *he's* not afraid."

Another way in which feelings are often invalidated is by implying that they must be reasonable or understandable or explainable. I commonly hear such expressions as, "But *why* do you feel that way?" or "There's no *reason* for you to feel that way," or "It doesn't do any good to feel that way." Feelings have an independent reality entirely apart from their causes, origins, reasons, or effects. When family members come to recognize the independent reality and validity of feelings, I see them giving more strokes and validation and acceptance to one another and resolving their conflicts in more healing ways.

For example, Gail says, "I feel afraid when you drive so fast." Robert misses the point if he responds with, "You drive just as fast," or "I'm not driving fast," or "I'm being careful." These answers focus on the *content* of the communication. Much more important is what is going on in terms of the *relationship*. In the relationship, Robert here has an opportunity to focus on Gail's fear, her pain. Whatever her reasons for feeling afraid, she feels afraid. She hurts. This is an opportunity for him to respond empathically to her pain, not pityingly, and not in order to take charge of her pain or be responsible for its quick diminution, but simply to let her know that her cry of pain has been heard, is cared about, and is recognized as real, and that she is supported in the way she chooses, in her wisdom, to deal with the real feeling.

Owning Feelings

I want to make one more point about feelings. In my perception, families and other human systems function best when their members "own" their own feelings. When I say "own," I mean two things: first, that they are open in expressing their feelings; second, that they do not attribute these feelings to anybody else.

The best argument I know of for openness in expressing feelings is presented by Sidney Jourard in *The Transparent Self*. All I would add to his statement is my perception that families and other human systems become more functional and less pain-ridden as their members become more open in their expression of feelings.

The second meaning of "owning" here is acknowledging my feelings as being my own. I see a seemingly endless array of devices that people use to try to put the responsibility for feelings somewhere else. For instance, I hear people say, "You make me angry." I do not accept the assertion that anybody makes anybody else angry—or sad, or happy, or defensive, or anything. What I see is that the person who is feeling anger has had an experience to which his body responded with anger. That anger is the product of the angry person's life experience up to that moment. The anger has meaning for the angry person in the light of his or her previous experience. In a sense, he or she has learned to "need" the anger, just as his or her body needs the sensation of pain to signal the brain to avoid destructive heat. It is my experience that the same kind of stimulus provided by the same antagonist to another person might not trigger anger as it does in this person. Moreover, it often happens that the same kind of provocation provided by the same antagonist to this very person on another occasion will not trigger anger. Such evidence satisfies me that "You make me angry" is not true. You don't do it to me. You do what you do. What you do is an experience for me. What I do with the experience is what I do, not what you do. I own it.

The effect of this realization can be very powerful. I see clients in therapy change from losers to winners when they grasp this idea. The difference seems to be that if you can make me angry (sad, helpless, loving, etc), you hold power over me. I am or can be your victim. The power is "out there." If I *own* the feeling, however, acknowledging that my experience of you is mine, and that I have power to use and see that experience in other ways, then I no longer give you the power to "push my buttons." The power is mine. I'm not a victim. Gone is the old feeling of helplessness and rage and possibly depression. I am a winner.

Let's apply this perception to three commonly expressed feelings: jealousy, trust, and embarrassment.

Jealousy/Trust/Mistrust

My partner says to me, "When I see the many personable women with whom you work in your occupation, I feel terrible pangs of jealousy." Then she hastens to add, "I want you to hear very clearly that I am not putting this on you. I do not want you to take it on. And I am not making a request for a behavior change. I'm telling you this because I want you to know me intimately, and these jealous feelings are part of my intimate self." What a warm message that is: open, honest, sharing, trusting. Had she implied in any way that I was the cause of her jealousy or that I was "doing it to her," much of the love message would have been missing from her communication. Blame would have taken its place. I could easily have become defensive, thus closing myself to her, and might even have counterattacked with blame and recrimination. Instead, by owning her feelings, she made it easier for us to draw closer together, and did herself the favor of keeping her eye on the feelings of insecurity that underlie jealousy.

As self-esteem rises, jealousy diminishes. As we learn to be less needful of others for our feelings of worth, we can free ourselves from the pangs of jealousy.

Sometimes the consequences of a pain like jealousy can be destructive. If I let my jealousy turn into suspicion and mistrust, and if, in fact, your behavior gives no real ground for me to feel suspicious or distrustful, then we are both losing. I lose in feeling the pain of my jealousy, suspicion, and mistrust. You lose in feeling the pain born of being falsely perceived, not truly known to your partner.

For the object of mistrust, the pain can be intensified if it is accompanied by blame or withdrawal. I hear parents express mistrust toward teenage children as though the power were "out there." The parent says, "I don't trust you to drive the car carefully" or "I don't trust your choice of friends." Too often the implied message is, "I am the judge of your trustworthiness. You are untrustworthy, and I want you to try to prove to me that you are trustworthy." Most teenagers are quick to pick up this implication. The inference they draw is, "My parent is putting a control trip on me, in which I have to try endlessly to get a judgment in my favor, and I have no confidence that I have an impartial judge."

I see something similar when I hear a wife, for example, say to her husband, "Since you had that affair with your secretary, I just don't trust you when you come home late." The response to such a statement will probably be defensive (e.g., "But that was twelve years ago, and there hasn't been anything like it since"), and the reply will then be accusatory (e.g., "You say there haven't been any others, but how do I know?").

The parties involved in such a transaction tend to assume that the transaction is about whether the accused person can prove that he or she is to be trusted. Proceeding on that assumption is a loser's course for both parties. It sets up one as the judge of the other's integrity. The victim perceives that he or she comes out as a loser, no matter what he or she does. If I question your trustworthiness, that sets up a condition of inequality in the relationship, in which I am both accuser and judge. The result is a severe strain on the relationship, and a certain emotional distance between us. If, instead, you don't try to prove your trustworthiness to me, you risk the continuance of my mistrust and the resulting distance in the relationship.

I want to get away from those binds and impasses. If I am having a problem in my relationship with you, I want to tell you about it. I want to feel trust for you, but I am aware that I don't feel trust; so something vital to the relationship is lacking for me. I don't want you to hear this as an accusation or a putdown. I'm owning it as my problem, and I would like you to give me your love and empathy and active listening as I work on this problem. Perhaps I have been conditioned in my life to have difficulty trusting anyone (or trusting men, or women, or authority figures, or whatever), or to expect people to make no mistakes and to mistrust them forever if they make even one mistake. Or perhaps I am picking up from you some signals, so subtle that I'm not even aware of what they are, that feed my feelings of mistrust. My guess is that if I can give you that kind of owning message in the relationship in which you and I are intimately related, we'll have a good chance of either restoring trust or finding out that trust is indeed not warranted. Either outcome seems preferable to the long-continued, unresolved feelings of mistrust that corrupt and corrode relationships in which the parties don't own their feelings of mistrust.

Embarrassment

Embarrassment is another feeling often ascribed to another person. When the person feeling the embarrassment can remember to own it, he or she keeps the power over that feeling and over the expressions of that feeling, and can enrich the relationship in which the feeling is expressed. For example, if you say to me, "You embarrassed me in front of all those people," I am likely to respond defensively with, "Why, what did I do?" From that inauspicious beginning we have the makings of a fight without resolution, in which one blames and accuses, and the other defends and excuses. Instead, there are several far more attractive options. One option is to own the feeling without even making any request for change of behavior. In exercising that option, my words might be, "When you get drunk at a party and tell stories for 45 minutes, I see people trying to get away from you, and I feel embarrassed. I realize that the way they see you is not my problem—it's yours or theirs—but emotionally I take it on. I want you to hear that I'm not requesting any change in your behavior, and I'm not trying to put you down. I just want to share with you the feelings I've expressed as my own."

The Power of "I Want" and "No"

The solutions proposed in Parts Two and Three for resolving conflicts depend on straight, clear communication, for which clear statements of "I want" and "no" and "yes" are essential. Clarity in these communications appears to correlate with self-esteem, that is, with the self-perception that I deserve and have a right to say what I want and do not want, to have whatever feelings I have, and to express my wants and needs and feelings, and that I do not need to meet the wants and needs and feelings of others, even though I may care deeply about them all. I do not count myself out. I do not count you out. I count us both in. We both win.

Time after time, in working with dysfunctional families, I see the ambiguity and confusion brought about by unclarity in expressing wants and refusals. Richard is a househusband who used to call his family to dinner with the words, "Are you ready for dinner now?" He expected other family members to treat those words as a call to come to dinner. They seldom did so. His reaction was one of disappointment and anger. When he recognized the ambiguity of his words, he changed the call to, "Would you please come to dinner now?" I cannot report that everybody came promptly to dinner forever after, but he enjoyed far more success than before, and failures to respond as expected could be more clearly and less contentiously dealt with.

In another family, Ruth followed the custom of asking Steve, "Would you like to eat out tonight?" He would usually say no. She would then prepare and serve dinner with an air of injury and silent hostility. In counseling, it was revealed that she intended her question to mean that she would like to eat out, and that she expected Steve to understand her words as a request, rarely made, to relieve her of preparing dinner. On hearing this revelation for the first time during counseling, Steve expressed surprise at this interpretation of the words, remorse and sorrow at having been unaware of her need for relief, and willingness to comply with her wishes. When Ruth learned to say clearly, "Would you please go out to dinner with me tonight?" or "I would appreciate your going out to dinner with me tonight," or "I would like you to take me to dinner tonight," the miscommunication disappeared. (Incidentally, the frequency of her desire to eat out also diminished.)

Not all uses of "I want" are as simple and as comfortable as in these two examples, nor are all conflicts as easy to resolve. Consider situations in which one marital partner says to the other, "I want our children to be brought up in my faith, not yours," or "I don't want children, even though I know it is important to you to have a large family." Even with the utmost love, the clearest communication, and the soundest self-esteem on the part of both partners, the relationship could founder on differences of such gravity. I am therefore not saying that a clearly stated "I want" will produce the hoped for miracle every time. I do say, however, that the chances are better when "I want" is clearly and compassionately and appropriately expressed than when it isn't.

In reality, to make a request is not to impose on anyone. To make a request is to put oneself clearly in the relationship. It gives important information about the sender to the receiver of the request. In a truly clear and straight relationship, the sender of the request recognizes that the receiver has the right to say no or yes, or to make a counterproposal, or to ask for more time or information. If the receiver says "no," that "no" is simply an "I want" in negative form. It also contributes important information in the relationship. In response, the maker of the request may seek additional information, or give additional information, or make or invite counterproposals. Persuasion, at these times, is counterproductive. It is most often experienced as exerting pressure, stopping communication, and creating the perception of a one-up/one-down relationship. On the other hand, it is vital to make clear the importance that the requester or refuser attaches to the request or refusal, including the intensity of all feelings.

Guilt so often gets in the way of clear statements of "I want" and "no" that I want to say a few words here about guilt.

Guilt

I see guilt as a corrosive and destructive force. It takes many forms. Joe felt guilty every time he enjoyed himself sexually with his wife. Marie came to me for counseling because she experienced feelings of guilt whenever she bought attractive clothing for herself. Charlie, whose comrades died in a battle near him, felt guilty for having survived.

I use the word guilt to mean something different from regret, remorse, or contrition. Guilt is a judgment of self-blame or self-condemnation leveled against the doer of the deed; whereas regret is an evaluation of the deed itself, coupled with the doer's feelings of pain, loss, anxiety, sorrow, or related feelings on recognizing the negative effects of the deed. I think of regret as accompanying a judgment made in the internal Adult (see Appendix A, Item 1). Guilt is the product of judgments that were made by parent figures in the individual's life and that have been internalized uncritically by the individual.

Once a young bride was preparing her first roast for her husband. On seeing her cut off the tip of the roast before placing it in the pan, her husband inquired why that was done.

"That's what you're supposed to do with a roast," she said.

"But why?"

"I don't know exactly, but Mother always did."

"But why?"

"I don't know. Let's call Mom and find out."

So they did, and Mother's replies were similar to those of her daughter: that was the way *her* mother did it.

So they called Grandmother: "Grandma, why are you supposed to cut off the tip of the roast before you put it in the pan?"

"Oh, I wouldn't say you're *supposed* to. I always did it because my pan was too small."

The fable dramatizes how guilt is bred and fed. When you are a little person, you don't have very much information on how to make your life and your actions effective and safe. You try to learn how to do this by observing the behavior and listening to the words of the significant adults in your life. You're inclined to accept their values as The Truth, because you don't have comparative information against which to weigh and measure these values. In the early days of your life, you accumulate a sizeable body of these "truths" and act on them uncritically because you lack either the information or the maturity to question them. Then you internalize them and embed them in the internal Parent. In later years— sometimes as early as age five, but almost certainly by age thirteen for most individuals—you have accumulated a large body of information that would be useful to you for questioning the values that you earlier internalized uncritically; however, it seldom occurs to you to question some of those values, because you've put them into the dark recesses of the internal Parent where information is stored that no longer seems open to question.*

In the case of Joe, who felt guilty for enjoying sexual experiences with his wife, the relief of his distressing situation came when he was able to

---

*For an in-depth examination of how these value systems are formed and flourish, see Claude Steiner, *Scripts People Live*.

separate his parents' disapproval of sexual enjoyment from his own values, based on his own experience.

Marie, who felt guilty about buying attractive clothing for herself, was able, in counseling, to remember indirect, subtle messages from her father that she should not ever compete with her well-dressed mother. She loved her father very much, but saw her mother repeatedly put him down and humiliate him. It became important for her to make her father right in as many ways as she could. In counseling she came to realize that one way in which she had chosen to make him right was by accepting his indirectly expressed value that she should not be well-dressed—or so she perceived the expression of his value. She came to see her guily feeling as a way of continuing to make her father "right." Seeing this, she was able to give it up.

The case of Charlie, who felt guilty for having survived battles in which his buddies died or were maimed, is more complicated. His memories were that his parents had decided that his older brother was a genius and was to have a college education, no matter what sacrifice was required of the other family members. And the sacrifices were great. The family income was low, and the most spartan rules prevailed in the home: rules against the making or eating of candy, against purchasing admissions to amusements, against the avoidable uses of light and water, against replacement of even threadbare clothing. The message perceived by this little person growing up was that it was wrong for him to use his life for any purpose other than the support and advancement of his brother (Buddy). This value he internalized as though it were eternal Truth, and then applied inappropriately to convict himself of guilt for still having his own life instead of devoting it to the maintenance of his buddies' lives.

When I go back inside myself to my early growing-up days, I can get in touch, all over again, with the realization that I am very small, that there are a lot of things I don't know, that many of these things are perceived as dangerous, that my parents are big and strong and wise and knowledgeable and have answers to things, and that it is good to be able to depend on them. It would be intolerably scary not to be able to depend on them; so I make them utterly dependable by not looking at the possibility that they might be wrong or fallible or weak. I make them right. I internalize their "rightness" as the Truth, and close the door to any further examination of the rightness or wrongness of the parental values. That accumulation of internalized values becomes my value system, even after I have acquired enough additional information, maturity, and competence to be able to reexamine those values and reject the ones that do not actually fit me.

Feelings of guilt are corrosive and destructive because they constitute continuous self-condemnation hurled by the internal Parent over and over again, in effect saying, "You're not O.K. You're not O.K. You're not

O.K." The damage to self-esteem can be severe; and, since the judgments are inappropriate to the person's own life and time, they damage the person's relationships and self-esteem alike.

Guilt Distinguished from Regret

Whereas guilt represents the internalized value system of another person acquired during the individual's early years, regret (or remorse, or contrition) consists of judgements made not by the internal Critical Parent, but by the internal Adult. For example, if I do a thoughtless act and find later that the act has caused you pain, the guilt message from my Critical Parent may be something like, "You are a bad person for causing pain to another individual." The message from my Adult might be something like, "What you've done has caused pain to someone you care about. With a little more attention to the facts, you might have avoided this result. You sincerely regret the misjudgment and the painful result. This can be a learning experience for you. Now it might be appropriate to take steps to ameliorate the other person's pain if you choose to do so."

The guilt message is a message that says I lack worth. The regret message is not a judgment about my worthwhileness at all; it is an evaluation of my behavior. The guilt message lowers self-esteem. The regret message, in contrast, can add to my sense of competence and worth.

3

Choosing a Mate, and
Choosing Parents

PROBABLY THE BEST REMEDY for family conflicts is to choose your partner (or partners) wisely in the first place. Functional relationships consist of compatible individuals who can respect themselves and other family members. They do not distort their transactions with other family members by resorting to defensiveness, destructive scripts, misperceptions, guilt, or blame.

I am not saying that these individuals will not have conflicts. I cannot imagine a real human relationship without conflict. Successful relationships are not those that are free from conflict, because there are no such relationships. Successful relationships are those in which the members find how to resolve conflicts in ways that strengthen the relationship rather than damage it.

How can successful relationships be formed? What are some criteria for success in relationships? Let's list a few guidelines quickly, then go back and pay special attention to the more significant ones.

Checklist for Mate Selection

Love is important in a relationship. In the present-day society with which I am familiar, it constitutes perhaps the strongest reason for forming and maintaining a relationship. Love alone, however, is an inadequate foundation on which to base a relationship. Love exists in the internal Child; the judgment about whether a relationship will be good for its members is made not in the Child but in the Adult. There are criteria that the Adult can use in deciding whether the loved person will be a good partner. Some questions that may be asked about the prospective partner are the following.

Is the prospective partner the kind of person who will support and enhance the self-esteem of the other family members?

Will the candidate make space in the relationship for the self-motivated growth and change of all family members?

Does the prospective partner accept you unconditionally as you are, and not expect you to change to suit his or her wishes?

Will the prospective partner send and receive undistorted communication?

Will the prospective partner be aware of and express feelings, thoughts, and emotions freely, and encourage such expression in other family members?

Does the prospective partner have enough self-esteem to be able to "own" her or his feelings, wants, and perceptions?

Is the prospective partner one who will engage, and permit other family members to engage, in easy changes between active and passive, leader and follower, dependent and independent and interdependent?

Will the prospective partner be able to withstand stresses during the course of the relationship?

Is there sexual attraction?

Do the prospective partner's values and expectations coincide with yours in areas in which differences (e.g., what the religious orientation of the children is to be) would likely result in conflict and alienation?

Are your differences such that they complement one another (e.g., such that one partner can be "on stage' at a party, and the other partner be an appreciative audience)?

Now let's take a closer look.

Criteria for Choosing Partners

Love

One of the difficulties in choosing a partner wisely is that love gets in the way. I may "fall in love" with a girl because of the way she wrinkles her nose, loves to dance, giggles as though she is being tickled, and enjoys the many ways I touch her body. But these delights, which appeal to my internal Child, tell me nothing about whether this lovely candidate can give unconditional positive regard to the way I sometimes fear to confront a client, or to my occasional feelings of inadequacy as a male, or to my forgetting important dates, or to my tendency sometimes to use authoritarian methods in trying to cope with young children.

Making the whole matter even more difficult is a mythology that our culture has accumulated about love. It is said that there is mature love and there is immature love. Immature love is sometimes referred to as puppy love, sometimes as infatuation. Mature love, on the other hand, is supposed to be the kind that will assure the success of a relationship. The problem with this test of mature love is that we never know whether love is mature until after we have discovered whether the relationship has been successful. When we are in the throes of the love feelings, we are inclined to characterize them as mature. If the relationship then flounders, we're likely to look back and say that it was not mature love, but infatuation. So love as a test for forming a relationship or choosing a partner seems not very reliable at the point when we are doing the choosing.

For me, this problem does not at all negate the value of love. Love is good bcause it feels good. Love is good because, under the influence of love, we are likely to feel more OK than without it, and we are likely to make our partners more OK. Love is good for as many reasons as there are people who love. Love is good simply because love is. What is in the Child—joy, sorrow, pain, delight, rebellion, love, etc.—is a part of the universe in which we live, like the law of gravity or the existence of the sun and the planets. We can fight it (and be losers), or we can accept and choose it (and be winners), making it our own. So we can accept and choose love when we feel it simply because it is. But to use love as indicating, by itself, that the loved person is a good candidate for partnership in an ongoing relationship is to rely on a very unreliable measure.

The choosing of a partner is a task not of the internal Child, which feels love, but of the internal Adult, which takes in information, processes it to discover its significance for our survival, and makes choices based on the available information, including information from the Child who is in love. Here are some of the criteria that our internal Adult can use in choosing partners.

Enhancement of Individual Self-Esteem

In my judgment, the most important function for a family, and the most important prerequisite for a family's success, is that it support and, if possible, elevate the self-esteem of each of its individual members. For that reason the first question in choosing a partner must be: Is this the kind of person who will enhance my self-esteem and the self-esteem of present or future members of the relationship? Is this the kind of person who will keep in mind, during conflicts, the importance of making sure that everybody in the relationship wins? Does this person send the basic message "I'm OK, you're OK"?

In my experience, a person can send OK messages to others when that person feels basically OK about himself or herself. The more defensive a person is, the more difficult it will be for him or her to hear other family members without distortion and to make them right.

Leeway for Growth and Change

To be accepted and chosen just as I am is important to me in a relationship. It is essential to my health that I have a partner who enhances my self-esteem by continuing to choose me unconditionally just as I am. It is equally important that my partner's acceptance of me not be conditional on my staying as I am. Healthy individuals grow and change. A nurturing relationship is one that accepts and supports change and growth in its members. Change and growth in any family member puts a certain amount of strain on the relationship, requiring the other family members to adapt to the change. So in choosing a partner I need to make sure that I choose someone who can adapt to my changes and who can give me unconditional acceptance as I have become, even though that is not the way I was. One writer has said: "Love is giving another person the space to be just the way they are—and the way they are not."

There is a limit to any person's ability to give advance approval to changes that other family members may make. When I make my changes and you see what those changes are, you may not like them. You may not like the person that I have then become. Moreover, in your process of change, the person that you originally chose may cease to be acceptable to the person that you have become. So you cannot reliably promise in advance to okay me no matter how I may change. In choosing you as my partner, therefore, I don't ask for assurance that you will okay me for all time, no matter what. I look only to see whether you are right now a person who is open to growth in yourself and in me.

Expectation of Change

Although I do want my partner to support and encourage whatever changes I choose for myself, I do not want my partner to indicate in any way that I ought to change, or that it would be good for me to change, or that my partner would love me more if I changed. These messages carry the implication that I am not OK as I am and that my partner's love for me is conditional, and they could contribute to lower self-esteem.

One of the saddest self-delusions is that the prospective partner will change in the direction that you would like. It is true that both you and your partner will change. It is not true that you can predict the rate or direction of change. And it undermines the relationship to expect your partner to overcome those characteristics that you now find unacceptable. Choosing a partner in the hope that these unacceptable qualities will change is a conditional acceptance of the person. A conditional acceptance is a rejection. The message is, "I accept you except for these areas, and in them I reject you." A rejection or conditional acceptance undermines the other person's self-esteem. His or her internal Child is likely to resent and rebel against the implied command to change. This makes the desired change even less likely. The result, for the partner who desires the change in the other, is likely to be disappointment and resentment.

Undistorted Communication

If you say to me, "I would like to buy this book," but I translate your statement into, "I want you to buy this book for me," there is a distortion in our communication. In dysfunctional families, there are many such distortions. In functional families there are relatively few.

I may distort your communication because I have learned to do so in the relationships that have constituted my experience from the time of my birth until now. In the example just given, I hear your expressed intention as a demand on me. In all likelihood, I learned in growing up that parent figures in my life intended their apparently simple declarations as demands—or, at least, so they seemed to me. If they were indeed intended as demands, and if I failed to hear the demand implicit in the statement, my world would have been uncomfortable. So learning to hear the implied demand was an exercise in intelligence, and helped me survive relatively comfortably in the environment in which I found myself. In my new relationship, I will be inclined to apply that learning in ways that have always worked for me in the past. That is, I will tend to translate simple declarations into implied demands. In the new relationship, however, that translation may be a distortion of the actual communication.

Just about everybody tends to distort some communications because of patterns learned from previous experience that are being incorrectly applied to the present situation. To find a partner who never distorts is probably too much to hope for. What your Adult can do, however, is to spend enough time with the prospective partner to see how much distortion goes on, and whether you can accept, tolerate, and cope with that much distortion.

Distortion may occur not only in hearing the communications sent by another partner, but also in the way communications are sent. For example, if I say, "Would you like to go to a movie tonight?" I am not saying, "I would like to go to a movie tonight." If I *intend* to say, "I would like to go to a movie tonight," it is a distortion to say, "Would you like to go to a movie tonight?"

This is a very simple example. Distortions become more complicated and grave when they touch more deeply our inner feelings, particularly those concerned with self-image and self-esteem. Signals that some of these feelings are at stake can be heard in such cries of pain as, "If you really loved me, you would *know* that's what I meant," or "But it just isn't my way to express feelings in words," or "You always . . .," or "You never . . . ."

Discrepancy. Another kind of distorted communication is the so-called discrepant communication. For example, the sender of the message has tightened his hands into fists, is red in the face, is clamping his jaws, and gives other body messages that he is angry, but says in a tight voice that he is *not* angry. Discrepant messages are particularly disturbing to children, but also have crazy-making effects on adults.

Incongruency. A related form of distorted communication is the incongruent message. In incongruent messages, the sender's message does not match the sender's real feeling. A guest negligently breaks a rare antique of yours. Your heart sinks, and you are angry, but you smile and tell the guest not to worry about it. You mask your real feelings; you are incongruent.

> *Incongruent:* Not consistent with sender's feelings.
> *Discrepant:* Not consistent with other messages from the sender.

Double binds. The "double bind" is another kind of distorted communication. An example of a double bind is when Father gives Son two neckties for his birthday; Son proudly puts on one necktie; and Father says disappointedly, "You didn't like the other one?" Son may perceive the situation as one in which he cannot win. If double binding by one or more members of the family is frequent, and if the family also follows a "rule" of not commenting about the no-win nature of the communication, the crazy-making effects can be devastating, particularly if the individual perceives the relationship to be vital for his or her survival.*

---

*For a more detailed discussion of communication, see Chapters 4 and 5.

Owning. One aspect of undistorted communication is called *owning.* I use the word owning in several ways.

One way of owning in a communication is to say clearly what I want. If I want you to come to bed and turn off the light now, it is important for me to say clearly to you that I want you to come to bed and turn off the light now. I do not own my want if I say, for example, "Are you ready to come to bed and turn off the light now?" If your answer is "No," you are simply saying that you are not ready. Because of my indirectness, however, I have opened the way for myself to hear you rejecting my request. In fact, I have not made a request, although I may have intended a request. I have done no more than ask you if you are ready. The transaction is simpler, more direct, and less distorted if I own my want by saying clearly that I want and what I want.

If I make a request of you, one of your optional answers is "No." No is an important kind of owning. If you mean no but say something other than no, you are distorting communication.

Another kind of owning is owning feelings (see Chapter 2). If I am disappointed because you forgot my birthday, I do not own my feelings by saying, "If you loved me, you would have remembered my birthday." I do own my feelings if I say, "I'm disappointed that you didn't remember my birthday." In owning my feelings in that way, I make a gift to the relationship. The gift consists of vital information about that part of me and the relationship that exists in my feelings. If instead I send words of blame, the effect is to "make you wrong" and to undermine your self-esteem and the relationship.

Another kind of owning is to label my perceptions of you, or my guesses about you, as my own. For example, if I say, "You don't really mean that," I am engaging in mind reading about your intentions. It would be more accurate to say, "I don't believe that you really mean that." Similarly, if I say, "Your words show me that you are angry with me," I am not owning my perception. It is more accurate to say, "From your words I perceive that you are angry with me."

Expression of Feelings

In observing well-functioning families, I notice over and over again that feelings, thoughts, perceptions, and attitudes are freely and openly expressed. There are few, if any, taboo subjects. There are few forbidden words. The verbal expression of anger is accepted as healthy. Boys are not told that men are not afraid; they learn that people who feel fear can properly express fear.

If your prospective partner has not been encouraged, in growing up, to be aware of and to express feelings, all is not lost. He or she can learn to become aware of feelings and to express them. This will probably require time and patience, because the person must learn not only a new awareness and a new vocabulary, but also that it is safe, in the environment you provide, to speak freely in these formerly taboo areas.*

Sexual Attraction

In most relationships between marital partners, sexual attraction is held to be important, even essential. This appears to be true even with couples who, for a variety of reasons (e.g., physical impairment), have agreed to forgo sexual intercourse. "Good sex" can increase feelings of closeness and mutual importance. Like love, however, sexual attraction can blind the partners to the need to use more Adult criteria in choosing mates.

Sexual attraction can also lead to discord and alienation. If one partner seeks sexual gratification when the other does not want to participate or if sex is used as a way of sweeping problems under the rug, the relationship will suffer.

Sexual activity is best when it is part of a total pattern of caring, sensitivity, and straight, open communication.

Interdependency

In choosing a partner for yourself, it is a good idea to look at whether the candidate's pattern of dependence and independence fits with your own. For example, if you want a relationship in which you can comfortably be the domestic person who doesn't know one end of a hammer from the other, and in which you can depend on your partner to make a living for the two of you, you will probably be quite uncomfortable with a partner who wants both of you to work and earn and use a hammer.

Expectations about dependence and interdependence are expressed in many ways. Are the cooking and dishwashing to be done by both partners together, or are those chores to be assigned according to male-female roles, or in some other pattern? Is one partner to be the leader in pursuing a social life? Will one or both parents exercise discipline over the children? Which partner gets the new car, and which one gets the older car?

It has been my observation that in functional families each partner is sometimes active, sometimes passive, sometimes the initiator, and sometimes the follower. In functional families there appears to be freedom to redefine roles and relationships.

P.S.: To the Unhappy Child in Love Whose Adult Says the Loved One Would Not Fit You

---

*For a more complete discussion of feelings, see Chapter 2.

If you are in love, every nerve tingling joyfully when you are in the presence of the loved one, wanting to be with that person, and wanting some way to assure yourself that these lovely feelings will continue forever, what is to be done when your internal Adult says clearly, "You and the object of your love would not fit, would not be a good match"? At such times the internal Child is likely to experience terrible pain, loss, grief, and sadness. There may also be a surge of angry rebellion against the inexorable logic of the Adult.

This is a time for the nurturing Parent to make itself felt. If I am experiencing pain, sorrow, and anger in my Child, I naturally look for someone in whose arms I can take refuge and possibly find solace. The giving of refuge and solace is a function of the nurturing Parent. I can find that Parent either in another person or in myself, and possibly in both.

The parent figure I choose will not give advice, or tell me what to do, or even tell me what is right or wrong. And it will not try to diminish my anguish or my tears. My nurturing Parent will hear me fully and empathically. It will hear my frustration and my anger, if anger is there, and my rebellion, if rebellion is there. It will not reason with me about those things; it will simply hear me out and let me know, yes, for me to be having those feelings at this time is perfectly OK. It will not pass judgment on decisions that I make in either my Adult or my Child, though it may share its own experience and perceptions on the choices my Child is making. And as I hear my nurturing Parent feed back to me, I may become aware that I am hearing a very real and compassionate exercise in active listening, as discussed in Chapters 5 and 6.

Choosing Parents: Do You Qualify?

Often in my work I hear a client say through a cascade of tears, "My parents should never have had children." And it is not rare for a client to say to me, "If I had known then what I know now, I would not have had children." I have also heard judges, investigators, prosecuting attorneys, probation officers, and defense attorneys remark that there ought to be a way to prevent persons who neglect or abandon or batter children from having children.

I have never met or heard of any person on this Earth whom I would trust with the responsibility of saying who may and may not have children. I certainly do not feel qualified to do so, and would find it emotionally intolerable to make binding rules preventing this or that person from having children.

At the same time, I am appalled that, in this society, we have so few restraints—even from public education or counseling—on the complicated task of bringing up children and nurturing other family members to be happy, functional, adaptive individuals who are capable of love, understanding, and nondestructive patterns of social behavior.

My fantasy is that if children about to be born had adequate information on the qualifications of their parents-to-be, many of them—perhaps most—would elect not to be born to those parents or into that family.

Some children do have such a choise, when a parent is contemplating marriage or otherwise taking on a new partner, and gives her or his offspring a voice in the selection process.

To give those children a better chance to mature into healthy, well-functioning adults, I would like to recommend here some criteria that prospective parents could apply to themselves before undertaking to have the next child.

Feeling Good About Oneself

As I see it, the first requisite for successful and happy parenting is for the parent to feel good about herself or himself—"good" meaning "I'm OK, you're OK," as a basic life position. The parent who feels good about herself or himself is aware of and accepts his or her own feelings, emotions, sensations, thoughts, and characteristics as right just because they exist. (Feeling good about oneself is the equivalent of having high self-esteem, as defined in Chapter 2.)

Ability to Love

Closely related to the first requisite—the necessity for high self-esteem—is the ability to love others, to empathize with them, to intuit their moods and feelings, to accept and reinforce them just as they are, and to reflect back to them their basic all-rightness. The capacity to give children the love they need and to accept them as they are correlates directly with high self-esteem. Persons able to give love and acceptance are also likely to have had parent figures who were themselves able to give love and acceptance. Some people without that advantage learn to be good parents, but not without effort and pain.

Focused Attention

A third characteristic necessary for successful and gratifying parenting is the giving of focused attention to the child and to the child's wants, needs, thoughts, values, perceptions, feelings, emotions, health, and development. This requires not only genuine appreciation and interest, but also the will and ability to set aside the necessary time, time that is free enough from interruptions and distractions that one can give interested focus. By distractions I mean not only the pressure and intrusion of phone calls, clients, customers, working hours, and the like, but also the conflicting demands for attention from the other spouse, elderly parents, other children, and any other dependents, as well as distractions from the parent's own unmet wants and needs, e.g., distractions presented by the parent's ill-health, or by ongoing friction between the spouses, or by nervous or psychological distress.*

Straight Communication

The elements of straight communication are discussed at length early in this chapter and in Chapters 4 and 5. Communication is not just talk. It is the use of words, inflection and tone of voice, facial expression, body posture, silence, and other body signals to say clearly what is meant. It is also the ability to hear not only the message contained in the words, but also the entire message contained in the nonverbal communication, the context in which those messages are sent, the feeling state of the sender in sending the message, and the significance of the message to the relationship. Communication in this expanded sense requires more information, understanding, and skill than most of us have unless we practice. †

Consistency and Reinforcement

It is not only straight communication that requires patience and practice. Another art or skill requiring patience is the setting and enforcing of rules and the exercise of discipline (which is discussed more fully in Chapter 12). Here I want to say that a good rule must be definable, reasonable, and enforceable. The best of rules, however, will be subjected to testing. The testing of rules—even the breaking of rules—does not represent any lack of character or integrity or trustworthiness; it is a natural part of the child's makeup. It is a way of learning what a rule is. But even as we let the child know that it is not "bad" to test the rules, we have to make it clear that the rule means what it says, that we attach importance to it, that we will enforce it predictably, that we will reinforce desirable behavior, and that we will not reward undesirable behavior. Moreover, we will provide consistency

---

*See also the discussion of Building Self-Esteem in Chapter 1.

---

†Good communication is sometimes called leveling (See Virginia Satir, *Peoplemaking*) without blaming, placating, distracting, or retreating into ultra-reasonableness, and without resorting too often to the communication stoppers discussed in Chapter 5.

within the environment by modeling, in our own behavior, the kind of consistency, fairness, and responsibility that we expect of our children.

At the same time, we will not enforce a rule that we have come to see as mistaken or oppressive. We can model compassion, integrity, and fairness by having the strength to change.

When Not to Have Children

I would like to emphasize a few situations in which I have seen too many couples have children for the wrong reasons or at the wrong times, to the ultimate regret of themselves and their children. One of these is having a child in the hope that it will revitalize a failing marriage. This device almost never makes the marriage better, but instead adds another stress to an already overstressed situation.

Another wrong reason for having a child is to prove one's "manhood" or "womanhood," whatever that means. A man doesn't have to prove his manhood unless he is in doubt about it. A woman doesn't have to prove her womanhood unless she is in doubt about it. If a man is in doubt about his manhood, the sexual identity that he presents to his child is likely to be one of doubt, insecurity, ambiguity, and confusion. The same may be said about women. Prospective parents in this predicament would do better to clear up their doubts and insecurities before having children. The production of a new life does not remove the doubt, anyway, and the outcome is likely to be disappointment, frustration, resentment, and friction.

Another time not to have children is when there are already so many children in the family that the parents cannot give the focused attention that each child requires. A similar mistake is having a child when the family does not have enough financial resources to meet the needs of each child for food, shelter, health care, and safety. It is not true that children are "cheaper by the dozen." The price of this or that commodity may be less *per unit* when purchased in quantities, but the total price paid for the total number of units consumed rises with each new person added to the family.

Another wrong reason for having children is that "society" or our families expect us to do so. Children brought into the world for this reason too often feel themselves burdened for life with the resentments their parents feel for having yielded to this kind of pressure.

Yet another wrong reason for having children is the "cuddly baby" fantasy. Lots of young mothers and some young fathers think that "having babies" is the beginning of a perpetual pink cloud. The myth is that babies are cuddly and cute, that they will love their parents, that they will be grateful for the loving things that their parents do for them, that their various growth steps will be exciting, that they will fill the house with the sounds of laughter and the imagery of fresh perceptions, etc., etc.

Well, yes, but not quite. Having babies changes everything, not necessarily for the better. Parents can disagree bitterly about how to raise children, about what chores are whose responsibility, about whether the new mother is "overdramatizing" her fatigue and the pains in her back and her self-doubts about being a mother. Babies cost money, and these costs far exceed the tax advantages of having one more little exemption.

Babies can erode their parents' self-confidence, particularly with the first child. Everything is new; so many things that the new parents have never done or confronted before must be done right before this important little newcomer. But how do we do it right if we have never had any experience with it? And there are so many ways to do it wrong. And when the little being is in distress and we can't figure out what message it is sending, we are likely to feel inadequate, so much so that some parents actually resent the presence of the little someone who can inspire such feelings of low self-esteem.

Kids also break things. It is quite all right to say tolerantly that you can child-proof the house, and that kids need the leeway to break things in their necessary explorations and gratifications of natural curiosity. But when you see the valuable thing that they have broken, notwithstanding your best efforts and most loving acceptance, it is likely to feel like damage to something in yourself.

As though it were not enough to have inflicted willful damage, they may then lie about it. Yes, sometimes they do. And they take things that are not theirs. And they hit each other even though we don't believe in hitting. They can be expected to cheat and manipulate. They can be snobs and bullies. They can cherish values that we disdain, and disdain values that we cherish. There is no understanding their choices of friends and foods and clothes and things to play with or to swallow.

Often they smell. They get loud. Their parents' need for sleep on Sunday mornings and New Year's Day is of no concern to them. They may be rude to our friends and dangerously trusting of utter strangers.

They get colds and children's diseases just as their parents are about to take long-planned vacations or attend important social events. They develop facial tics, nailbiting, and other nervous symptoms that make you wonder what you've done wrong. They envy friends who have broken limbs, and sometimes seem bent on one-upping these heroes.

They can be utterly unreasonable. They don't know what appreciation is, and this blind spot may continue well into and beyond the teen years. As they grow, they are likely to become more assertive and more oblivious of our headaches, anxieties, financial limits, needs for love, and anything else that doesn't suit their wants.

Even the most loving couples can find, after a while, that they have forgotten the interesting things they used to talk about and do. Activities and words grow more and more child-centered, parent-centered. The spontaneous things you used to do, like grabbing each other sexually or yelling at each other angrily, now become more guarded or planned.

And then comes the day when, in your judgment, it is time for them to leave the nest, but they are stubbornly resistant. Or, even more painful, this untried nestling is determined to try its wings, blind, in your judgment, to the hazards of first flight. But whenever the parting time comes, whatever the circumstances, no matter how "right" the time may be, there is a heart-stopping wrench. Try as you might to retain your own center and to avoid coming to "need" your children or to be "needed" by them, the time for their going may be experienced as a kind of death even while it is an emancipation and relief.

So why do we do it? Hard to say. But I'd do it again.

PART TWO

Effective Communication and Active Listening

4

Getting Your Ideas Across: Increasing Your Listener's Receptiveness

LET'S LOOK FIRST at the high frustration level that accompanies virtually every unresolved conflict in an ongoing human relationship. I see husbands and wives screaming at each other. I see parents and children striking each other. I see sabotage in business organizations. I see teeth clamp, jaws work, knuckles whiten, faces redden, eyes avert, and shoulders slump. Sooner or later these nonverbal messages translate into frustration and rage, coupled with either resistance or surrender.

And what is this frustration all about? If you reflect on your own conflicts, whether at home, at work, in social clubs, or in other situations, you usually think your frustration is caused by the failure or refusal of another person to do what you want or need that person to do. Power thus appears to lie outside yourself, and you may feel powerless or helpless to get the other person to do what you want him or her to do.

Let's take an example. John comes home to his wife, Jane, at 8 P.M. Jane meets him at the door.

Jane: Are you aware of the time?

John: I'm aware of the time. It is precisely 7:57 on this watch for which you paid more than we can afford.

Jane: You get off work at 5, and here it is 8.

John: 7:57.

Jane: Not a word! Not a phone call! How am I supposed to know when to expect you home?

John: What does it matter? I can never count on you to be home when I get here anyway.

Jane: I'd be here more often when you get home if you'd be here on time.

John: I'd be home on time more often if you weren't always busy on jobs or taking classes.

Jane: You're so cold, so unfeeling.

John: Listen to Miss Frigid saying who's cold.

Jane: I'd be more responsive if you were less of an animal.

The *Content* of this particular transaction may or may not appear relevant to situations in your life, but probably much in the *Process* has a direct bearing on your success or failure in transactions with significant others in your life.

Using "Process" to Get What You Want

There is a vital reason for distinguishing between Content and Process, and this is it: conflicts are rarely solved in terms of Content, but seldom remain unresolved when Process is properly understood and employed.

To illustrate the difference between Content and Process, let's analyze the dialog between John and Jane in a tabular format. The Content is what they are saying on the surface. The Process is everything that is going on between them other than the content of what they are talking about. Although the process is obvious, the disputants ignore it.

Dialog	Content	Process
Jane: Are you aware of the time?	Time.	No feelings are expressed, although feelings in the relationship are what give the encounter significance.
John: I'm aware of the time. It is exactly 7:57 on this watch for which you paid more than we could afford.	Time, economy.	The retort about the time is sarcasm, evidently intended to wound Jane. Then a new issue is introduced, complicating the problem of resolution. Blame seems implied by the reference to the watch.

Dialog	Content	Process
Jane: You get off work at 5, and here it is 8.	Time and hours.	Here what is left unspoken is Jane's basic message that she is feeling hurt and left out.
John: 7:57.	Still the time of day.	John follows the unspoken agreement to keep the true gravity of the discussion hidden under the device of fact-finding about hours and minutes.
Jane: Not a word! Not a phone call! How am I to know when to expect you home?	The content is now enlarged to include Jane's expectations.	Jane's question about when to expect John home asserts by implication that there is a rule in their system that John would let her know when to expect him to return.
John: What does it matter? I can never count on you to be home when I get here anyway.	John shifts the content to his being unable to count on Jane.	John neither confirms nor denies the rule. He makes a defensive counter-charge.
Jane: I'd be here more often when you get home if you'd be here on time.	On-timeness in getting home continues as the content.	Jane defensively escalates the mutual blaming.
John: I'd be home on time more often if you weren't always busy on jobs or taking classes.	Same content.	The symmetric escalation continues. They are at an impasse. Still no feelings have been expressed. Neither one has said "I want" with any clarity.
Jane: You're so cold, so unfeeling.	Jane shifts the content to a characterization of John.	She makes the statement as though it were a truth about John instead of simply her perception of him at this moment. The effect is to put John down, and to increase his defensiveness.

Dialog	Content	Process
John: Listen to Miss Frigid saying who's cold.	Characterization of Jane.	Again, a symmetric escalation of hurting statements, this time attempting to match the other's derogatory characterization.
Jane: I'd be more responsive if you were less of an animal.	A new characterization of John.	The symmetric escalation continues; Jane now attempts to defend and justify her behavior as a reaction to John's behavior.

Looking at the overall process, the effect of this transaction has been alienating and distancing rather than bonding and healing. The frustration level in each appears to have risen appreciably. There have been many shifts in content, and as the discussion continues, issues of both content and process will probably become blurred, distorted, confused, and farther than ever from resolution. Neither participant has been at all effective in achieving, or even in getting closer to, what he or she wanted. In this state of ineffectiveness, each must have suffered a loss of self-esteem. With lowered self-esteem, defensiveness is the almost inescapable result. And as each becomes more defensive, his or her ability to heal the breach by giving a positive stroke to the other is diminished.

Using Process To Reduce Defensiveness and Frustration

How can the situation be changed for the better? Let's imagine the dialog between John and Jane as it might be if they were aware of their process, and relatively skilled at using it. Once again, we begin as John walks in at 8 P.M.

Dialog	Process
Jane: Oh, John, I have so many feelings about your coming home late that I can hardly sort them out.	She reports feelings, the intensity of her feelings, and her confusion about them. Her statement is direct right at the outset, her finger on the place where resolution is possible in the feelings bearing on the relationship.

Dialog	Process
John: (showing concern) I can tell you're upset; you're trembling, and you seem to have been crying.	He sticks to the subject with which Jane opened the transaction, i.e., Jane's feelings. He shows concern by his tone, his attention, and his posture. He gives her the vital information that he is aware of the various signs of her distress. This may be expected to have a healing effect.
Jane: I *am* upset. I kept going back and forth between being worried about you and being angry at you.	She begins to sort out her feelings. She owns them as her own without directing blame at John. This helps John to keep his attention on the subject of concern to her without becoming defensive and combative.
John: Jane, you thought something might have happened to me?	Jane has expressed both worry and anger. John chooses to emphasize worry rather than the anger, though he could have elected to deal first with the anger or to include both of Jane's feelings in his response.
Jane: Yes, and I don't want anything to happen to you; I want you here, safe with me.	John's nondefensive responses have enabled Jane to get in touch with the love that underlies both her worry and her anger. That love is, after all, the root and branch of their relationship.
John: Thank you for the gift of saying that.	He gives immediate, positive reinforcement for a response from Jane that he values.
Jane: But I'm not ready yet for a lovey-dovey talk! I'm just so angry I'm purple. When I think that you got off work at 5, and I didn't hear a word from you until 8 o'clock!	Even in the intensity of her anger—which she expresses directly and congruently with her feelings—she owns the feeling and does not translate it into blame, nor does she engage in fact-finding or cross-examination, either of which might well have led to a defensive response from John and a diminishing of Jane's effectiveness.

Dialog	Process
John: You were so hurt that I didn't let you know, and so worried about something happening to me, that you're just furious.	He stays with her feelings—which is what this transaction is about—rather than getting off into what happened. He sees that anger is a secondary emotion springing from other, more primary feelings, which he identifies as hurt and worry.
Jane: I *am* furious. I'd really like to hurt you in some way. It feels awful to say this, but I don't even trust you.	She continues to own her feelings without blaming or characterizing John.
John: Oh, that feels awful to me. I don't want trust to be weakened between us.	For the first time John shifts from Jane's feelings to his own. The risk in this is that if Jane does not yet feel satisfied that her own feelings have been fully expressed and heard, John's interposition of his feelings may produce a new subject for resolution before the first subject has been fully defined and accepted as an issue.
Jane: So let's deal with trust. What's going on between us?	She accepts the issue of trust. But her question is not "What happened?" which would have set her up as the judge of John's behavior and explanation, but "What's going on between us?" which is the issue with which both are now legitimately concerned.
John: The main thing going on between us, as I hear it, is that for you to trust me now, you need to know better how to predict my behavior, so that you can choose whether you want to be in this relationship.	He sticks to the here and now, and to the central issue of trust. He dares to identify the ongoing choice-making and risk-taking process, which is the very nature of an ongoing intimate relationship.
Jane: It's scary for me to hear you put it that way, but I guess that's	She joins in defining the issues and acknowledges her fear.

Dialog	Process
what it boils down to. What can I count on with you?	
John: You'll have to decide what you can count on, but I can tell you what I did and where I am now.	He does not fall into the trap of suggesting how Jane is to perceive his behavior. He leaves her the dignity of that choice. He offers a narrative of what he has done, not from the one-down position of being judged, but from a position of equality. In so doing, he takes the risk of whatever perceptions and conclusions Jane may draw.

Readers who like to know how the story ends—and particularly those who dote on happy endings—may be uncomfortable at leaving John and Jane at this unresolved point in their dialog. For those readers we will return to John and Jane in the chapter on conflict resolution. Our purpose here is not to look at the outcome, but to familiarize ourselves with process as a way of mastering the skills that we can apply in resolving conflicts, in heightening self-esteem, and in reducing the frustrations that bubble up from failing to get our ideas across and from failing to get what we want or need in our relationships.

Unfamiliarity of the Concept of Process

If you have experienced bewilderment, confusion, and even anger in trying to understand process by means of the unfolding dialog between John and Jane, you are in good company. When we teach classes on resolving family conflicts so that everybody wins, we see a lot of squirming, we get a lot of challenges, and we hear a lot of resistance. Some of this reaction is directed at the concept and application of process itself, because it is unfamiliar and bewildering to many. For example, when Jane says, "When I think that you got off work at 5, and I didn't hear a word from you until 8 o'clock," and John says, "You were so hurt that I didn't let you know, and so worried about something happening to me, that you're just furious," many class members laugh incredulously. They have had little or no experience with nondefensive responses, particularly with responses that arise from active listening or that indicate empathic concern for what the other person is saying. to them it would be much more credible for John to defend or justify his behavior, or to counterattack. Similarly when John says, "I can tell you're upset; you're trembling, and you seem to have been crying," doubters in our classes are inclined to brush his response aside, and to demand that he give a factual explanation of what he has been up to and why he is late. This would be a way to make John wrong (see Chapter 1).

To some class members, the notion, effectiveness, and language of process are so foreign and have so little connection with their previous experience that they drop out of the class. For those who remain, however, we begin, after a couple of weeks, to get messages of surprise (such as, "It works!") as class members begin to see the relative ineffectiveness of the old, familiar ways, and the new options for closeness, intimacy, and harmony that open up to them as they begin to develop skill in getting their ideas across in their intimate relationships.

What Do I Want?

Let's take a closer look at John and Jane. You yourself may have had similar experiences. You are at home awaiting the arrival of a belated family member. You experience successively doubt, anxiety, worry, fear, anger, resentment, and perhaps a host of other feelings. You may also associate this experience with memories of other incidents between you and this family member, and the feelings that were present at those times flood in on you again during this new experience. You may also associate the event with experiences you have had with other persons, pehaps going back into your childhood. Given all these dynamics, it is not easy (but also not impossible) to pause long enough to ask, "What do I really want right now?" If you greet the latecomer with angry accusations, the idea you are most likely to get across is that you want to hurt or punish the other person, to put him down, to make him wrong, or to put yourself in a one-up position.

Although these may be among your objectives, they are probably not usually your primary purposes. More likely, you want to express your upset and hurt, and you want some convincing expression that the other person cares about the feelings you have experienced and are experiencing. If these are the ideas that you want to get across, you are likely to be more effective if you abandon the blame game and pause a moment to ask yourself: what other methods might make me more effective in getting across the idea that this relationship is important to me, and that I want to be shown that I count for something in it?

Applying these words to the two-column dialog between John and Jane, and asking what idea they are trying to get across to each other, I perceive that each is acutely aware that they are talking about, and having an impact on, their *relationship* whether they mention that word or not. The basic idea that Jane in particular seems to be expressing is, "This relationship is important to me, and I want to know from you that I am important to you in this relatonship. When I say 'I', I mean my person, my feelings, my place in your life, my importance in the world."

We have not pursued the dialog far enough to get a clear picture of what John's basic idea is in this encounter. But I read this much in what he says in the second version of the dialog: "You matter to me enough in this relationship that I want to hear you completely and fully, and let you know that what I hear matters to me."

Apply this to your own life, in your recent encounters with other family members. Did you hear from the other family member, "This relationship is dear to me, and you are dear to me in the relationship"? If you had heard such a message, would it have made a difference in the encounter and in the relationship? Was your message to the other, "This relationship is dear to me, and you are dear to me in the relationship"? If it had been, might the outcome have been more to your liking?

In my work I hear a mother say about a son, "He keeps bad company, and we never hear a civil word out of him." And the son says about the mother, "She doesn't trust me to choose my own friends, and she turns everything I say into a lecture on how I should be different." This mother and son come into counseling and family therapy when their pain is so bad and the scars from their impasse so deep that despair pervades their transactions. From this unhappy position, many families (not all) make dramatic recoveries. Recovery generally takes place when the family members perceive that their pain grows out of frustration, out of a feeling of inability to get what they want, that what they basically want is to feel good about themselves and their world, and that for them to feel good about themselves and their world they need to feel effective in it, to be able to make sense of it, and to feel valued by the important others in it.

So this son needs to feel valued, not for what he does or how he behaves or what he has, but just for being as he basically is. And his mother has the same need. So somewhere along the path of recovery between this mother and son, she will probably have found a way of making him right by saying to him, perhaps not in these words but in various ways, "I am concerned for you because I value you. My experience tells me that there is danger to you in your choice of friends. But that's my experience, not yours. I offer my experience to you so that you can make it yours if you choose to do so. If you don't choose to do so, I respect that your power of choice for your life is basic to your being and to your existence, and I support your choice-making even when I fear the consequence of the choice you make." And the son will probably have found ways of saying to his mother in his own words, "I can see your concern for me, even though I resent what I see as your attempt to shape or control my choices. But I'm able to see that your need to push your experience onto me is a statement about yourself, your concern, your worry, your experience, and is not really a statement that I'm not OK. Your worry about my friends matters to me, and I would like to work out with you ways of making us both feel more secure about the friends I choose."

Relationships can be healed and enlivened by understanding and by applying the knowledge that the basic idea to get across in a relationship may not be the facts and blames—"what happened" and "who did what" and "you promised" and "I have a right"—but may instead be, "This relationship matters to me," and "You matter to me in the relationship." Let us see what we can discover about how to communicate that basic relationship message, in order to reduce the pain in family encounters and help all participants in family conflicts feel more effective, more worthwhile, more valued, and less defensive.

Focusing on Relationship

The message underlying the above examples is that: (1) there is an alternative to conventional ways of participating in family conflicts; (2) the conventional ways offer limited opportunity to resolve famly conflicts satisfactorily, because they do not address the basic idea of the importance of the relationship and of the members in the relationship; (3) the consequences of this omission are increasing pain, deepening frustration, lowered self-esteem, more rigid defensiveness, and an ever-diminishing openness to the love that is possible in relationships; and (4) the alternative is to keep the encounter focused on the central idea that "this relationship matters to me and you matter to me in the relationship."

To communicate that idea seems to me so important that I want first to make sure that we have the necessary skills in communicating generally.

Communication

Let's take a close look at what communication really is and how we can use it more effectively to get our idea across. Let's look at it in simple diagrammatic form. Let's say the "Sender" wants to send the message, "I want to do something for you that you will like." She can choose to encode her message in a number of forms. One form would be to express it in words; another would be to express it in actions. We will look at other forms in the course of this chapter, but for now let's say that a newly married woman lovingly selects for her husband a shirt in a color that his mother has said is his favorite. In placing that shirt before her husband, she is nonverbally communicating her message, "I want to do something for you that you will like" (Figure 4.1).

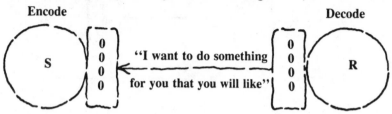

Fig. 4.1.

The husband (*R* in Figure 4.1) now decodes the message on the basis of his own experience. Unknown to his wife, his experience with that particular color has been that his mother persistently selected it for him over his repeated objections, and he perceives his wife's message as an attempt to establish with him the same kind of controlling relationship that he had with his mother.

If they do not talk about this, her perception that her selection for her husband is one of his favorites becomes true for her, and his perception that his wife is determined to play substitute mother becomes true for him. Later, if they go into counseling, one or the other may say to the counselor, "We never communicated about it." In actuality, they did communicate. their problem is that they did not communicate *effectively*. The wife communicated nonverbally by selecting a color that she thought would please her husband. He communicated with silence, which is almost always ambiguous. She decoded his silence as acceptance and confirmation of her uncommunicated assumption. This was the "process" of their transaction: the manner in which the messages were sent and received, the importance in the relationship, the antecedents of the transaction, the establishment of and adherence to the rule of silence.

Feedback

In this example, the Receiver could prevent a lot of present and future pain by using feedback, as in Figure 4.2. Feedback is a way for the Receiver to say, in effect, "This is the message I'm getting from you. Is that the message you are sending?" On the facts we have assumed, this Receiver would be saying in effect, "I'm assuming that you have selected this color in order to override my wishes. Is this true?" This gives the newly married couple an opportunity to make their motives

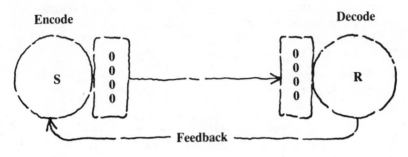

Fig. 4.2.

clear to each other, to clarify this particular transaction, and to establish the rule of openness and clarity in their relationship.

But it is likely that the wife has chosen to encode her message in more than just the act of putting a shirt before her husband. Let us assume that she has gone to the length of giftwrapping the shirt, enclosing a card declaring love, putting the package before him with a flourish, standing back with her hands clasped to see the result, looking intently at her husband, perhaps flushing, and smiling broadly. If the husband is alert to these many messages (i.e., if he is aware of process), he has much more to decode than we have reflected in the feedback assumed above. A more likely feedback for a Received attuned to process might be, in his own words, "I can see a lot of special preparation in this: the wrapping, the lovely card, the way you put the package before me and stand back, looking expectantly for my reaction. At the same time, my perception of these messages is distorted by the memory of my mother's pushing this color at me, ignoring my protests. So what I'm receiving is confused, and I'd like to know from you more clearly what you are sending."

The wife's face may fall, her disappointment may be great, but if she is as open and clear as her husband appears to be in this transaction, there is every reason to expect that they will achieve a happy outcome.

For our purpose, we have taken a beginning to look at communication and found it to be a complicated process. It may consist of words, actions, and context, as illustrated in the example we have chosen above. Let's attempt a more extended list.

Types of Messages; Forms of Encoding

Words. Words may be used to express or to obscure meaning. They do not always mean what they say. And they do not always mean the same thing to all participants. Alice and Hortense went to the movies every Friday night for thirteen years before they discovered that neither one had ever wanted to go. The series began when Alice said to Hortense, "Would you like to go to the movies tonight?" (Meaning intended: I assume that you would like to go to the movies tonight, and if that assumption is true I would like to do that for you.) Hortense answered, "OK." (Meaning intended: From your question I assume that you would like to go to the movies tonight, and if that's the case I would like to do that for you.) But the message intended by each was not the message perceived by the other, and the message received was not checked out. Similarly, parents complain that when they ask their teenagers what the teenagers have been doing, the answer is often, "Nothing." In counseling, the real meaning of "Nothing" may turn out to be, "I don't feel safe in telling you what I've really been doing," or it may be, "Your questioning where I have been seems to me like a violation of my self-concept as an emerging adult." Whether the words mean what they say or not, they are nevertheless an important means of communicating.

Inflection and Tone of Voice. Few of us can forget how important to us, as children, was the tone of voice of a parent figure in our lives in uttering a reprimand, asking a question, expressing concern, giving comfort, showing disappointment, or pretending interest. There is the obvious contrast of loud and soft. But loud may be loud with anger or loud with laughter. Soft may be soft tenderly or grievingly. I have heard tone of voice characterized as cold, steely, hard, threatening, hissing, biting, stroking, tender, bland, unconcerned, and many more. A Receiver who misses these aspects of communication is cutting himself or herself off from awareness of much information of value in the relationship. Similarly, a Sender who is unaware of how much is revealed in his or her tone of voice may be sending "crazy" messages, for example, by saying, "Of course I love you, dear," while the tone of voice says, "I couldn't care less."

Facial expression. For any Receiver who can see, facial expression is an important part of communication. One such expression is tears, which may mean anger, sadness, relief, or frustration, among other meanings. Another is laughter, which may be humorous, nervous, or relieved, or which may be intended to disqualify the other person. Among other facial expressions I think of narrowed, squinting eyes, tight lips, frowns, tight jaws, wide open mouth, sneering, lifting an eyebrow, or pouting. The Receiver cannot be sure of the true meanings of these messages without feeding back the message received.

Posture. Even an observer unfamiliar with the game of baseball can tell from the posture of an umpire and a player standing nose to nose that they are angry and are disagreeing emphatically. Similarly, the feelings of two lovers on a park bench can easily be inferred from the way their bodies bend toward each other and their hands reach out and touch. Most of us are alert also to a head held high (which may mean defiance), shoulders sagging (perhaps sorrow or discouragement), a long, quick stride (energy or determination), arms on hips, head thrust forward (blame or condemnation), the reaching out of arms and hands (loving, comforting, or grasping), and similar indicators.

I want to emphasize here that what I perceive, as the Receiver of the communication that you send in the form of body posture, is *my* perception based on *my* experience. It constitutes no more than an inference about your intent in sending that particular message in that particular form. If I attach importance (and I do) to making sure that the message I get is the same as the message you are sending, I will give you feedback about what I am receiving and will check with you to find out if that is the message you are sending. This same warning applies to all body expressions.

Other Body Expressions. Other body expressions include the rate and intensity of breathing, taut neck muscles, white knuckles, tight fists, physical striking, a tender pat, trembling, holding hands, blushing, turning pale, sweating, throwing up, and fainting, among others.

Silence. Communication theorists are fond of saying, "One cannot *not* communicate." Even silence is a communication. It is often an ambiguous communication, but it is a communication nonetheless. Often it has a punishing quality. Sometimes it seems tinged with fear, as with a child's refusal to respond to questioning. A particularly poignant characterization of silence as a communication is Phyllis McGinley's "A Choice of Weapons":

> Sticks and stones are hard on bones.
>   Aimed with angry art,
> Words can sting like anything.
>   But silence breaks the heart.

In Chapters 5 and 6, on active listening, we will explore ways of discovering the true message when it is encoded in the form of silence.

Absence, lateness. Failure or refusal to be present at an accustomed or promised time is often as ambiguous as silence. If the absence or lateness is attacked before the message is understood, serious miscommunication can result.

Context. The situation itself may give a separate meaning to the Sender's words or behavior. For example, a husband may say about his wife, "I see no value in living with her at all." The context, however, is that he is living with her. The words and the contxt taken together constitute a contradictory communication. Another example of the effect of context may be seen in the statement by the father of three young children, "Let's go to bed." If he is addressing his words to his wife, the message may be a sexual one in context. If, however, he is addressing them to his three young children, the same words usually have a parental quality in context. Similarly, the Sender's solemn word that he is contrite and intends to mend his behavior may be received one way the first time the message is sent, but quite another way when the message has been often sent and then disaffirmed.

Relationship. Relationship messages may be direct and obvious, as when one person says to another, "I love you" or "I hate you." Most often, however, relationship messages are tacit, implicit, indirect. For example, if we read the statement, "Stop talking; eat your spinach," we may infer that the Sender is a parent and the Receiver a child. The relationship message implicit in the statement is: my relationship with you is such that I have a right, or may be expected, to give you parental commands. The precise relationship is less clear if we read, "You're late. Where have you been?" We may guess that the Sender is the Receiver's employer or spouse or parent, but we can't be sure. What does seem implied by the statement is that the Sender is saying, "My relationship with you is such that I have a right, or may be expected, to call you to account about your time of arrival or, at any rate, to question you about it." It is highly unlikely that the Sender would be the Receiver's bus driver or mailman, much less a neighbor with whom the Receiver has never spoken. (We shall have much more to say about relationship messages in our discussions about conflicts among intimates, and of healing encounters as distinguished from alienating encounters, in Chapter 8.)

Using Multilevel Communication

The preceding discussion of the many levels of communication that can be and usually are sent simultaneously shows that the communication diagrams of Figures 4.1 and 4.2 are far too simple. Figure 4.3 more nearly represents reality, indicating as it does that the message sent is actually a combination of messages, some verbal, some not.

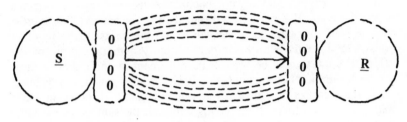

FIGURE 4.3.

If I understand and make use of this reality, I open up to myself both a number of options I can use to my advantage and a number of cautions to keep in mind, so that I won't limit or distort the effectiveness of my messages or of the messages I receive.

The opportunity that opens up to me is the opportunity to send effective messages, not only by means of words but also by means of many other devices: tones of voice, facial expression, posture, other body expressions, silence, context, absence and lateness, and relationships messages.

At the same time, I want to be on guard against distorting my communication by giving messages that are inconsistent with one another. For example, if I say, "I feel great," but my voice is flat, and my shoulders are sagging, I am giving discrepant messages. The result of the discrepancy may be to confuse the Receiver and impair my effectiveness.

As a Receiver rather than sender, I have a similar opportunity and a similar danger. On the opportunity side, if I am alert to the many messages being sent by the Sender—who may be unaware that she or he is sending some of them—I can pick up clues and meanings that would no be open to me if I were centering on the words alone. Conversely, if the messages are there for me to read, and I am not alert to them, I miss much of the meaning of the transaction and may be ignoring information that is vital to the strength of the relationship.

The principal device for securing these opportunities and avoiding these pitfalls in sending and receiving messages is feedback. Feedback is indicated diagrammatically in Figure 4.2 and has been discussed briefly in this chapter, but the power and effectiveness of the feedback device, and particularly of the feedback known as active listening, merit a closer look, which we will carry out in Chapters 5 and 6.

"Crazy-makers"

I remember a family therapy session in which the father addressed some words to his children through clenched teeth, the veins standing out on his forehead, his body bent forward menacingly, his hands gripping the arms of his chair so tightly that his knuckles were white. The whole family fell silent, each exhibiting fear. But the father denied that he was angry. This is a crazy-maker. It is called a discrepant communication; i.e., one part of the message (in this case, the body signs) does not match another part (in this case, the words). The origin of the discrepancy was the father's lack of congruence: the message did not match his true feelings. Young children are particularly sensitive to the inner feelings of the important others in their lives. When those feelings do not match the messages sent by those important others, the children may doubt their own perceptions and intuitions. Some children may conclude not merely that the messages are discrepant, but also that they themselves are out of touch with reality and are unable to make sense and order out of their world.

A related crazy-maker is this one:

Child: I'm hungry.

Parent: You can't be hungry. You just ate.

The implied message to the child is: Don't trust your own body awareness. I know your feeling better than you do.

Here is another one:

Child: I am afraid.

Parent: You're not afraid. There's nothing to be afraid of.

The implied message is: Don't trust your own awareness of your feelings. The feeling you're aware of is not based on reality. You are out of touch with reality.

Inconsistency may be a third kind of crazy-maker. If on some days I strictly enforce a rule against sweets before dinner but on other days I act as though there were no such rule, my children may have a hard time making sense and order out of their world.

Rules or words with obscure definitions may also be classed as crazy-makers. What am I really saying to my children when I leave them with a baby-sitter and warn them, "Now be good"? What guidelines are there for being good? Too often, the message may be received as: On pain of punishment you had better know in advance what behavior will be considered acceptable and what will not be acceptable, and you will be held accountable—as a bad person—if you guess wrong.

Ignoring strongly held feelings or strong demands for attention may be felt as crazy-makers. If I am a tearful wife or a strongly assertive child and I am ignored, I could begin to question whether I know how to function interpersonally, and I might begin to doubt that I am even here. Double binds are another kind of crazy-maker. An angry wife says to her meek husband, "For heaven's sake, be spontaneous." If he isn't spontaneous, he loses. But to be spontaneous on command is obviously impossible. He loses either way.

A husband says to his wife, "I'm not going to tolerate your being submissive any more; from now on the rule is that we're equal." If the wife does not assert equality, she loses with her husband. But to be equal in compliance with a rule that he has made unilaterally is impossible. She loses either way.

A parent says to a teenager, "We don't expect you to choose a career on the basis of our values, but if you continue with the work you are doing now, we will withdraw our support." If the teenager continues in the present direction, he or she loses parental support. But to continue to be supported, the teenager must abandon autonomously chosen work. He or she loses either way.

The classic definition of the double bind is a choice in which either alternative is a losing one for the victim, who furthermore perceives his or her survival to depend on the person who presents the choice. The victim can escape the crazy-making effects of the double bind by an amazingly simple device: make a process comment. An example of a process comment is: "When you present that choice to me, I don't see any way to win."

Another kind of crazy-maker is the double message. One father with whom I worked was distressed about his son's running away repeatedly. He had "tried everything," he said, to convince his son not to run away. But he had also regaled his family and his friends with amusing and exciting tales about his own running away during his growing-up days. The son was getting contradictory messages. In another family, the mother was unhappy about her teenage daughter's use of alcohol—and about her own compulsive use of alcohol. The example she set contradicted the teaching she was giving by another means. Another mother gave her son two different messages. One was, "Be a man." The other, said contemptuously and scornfully, was, "You're just like your father."

Parents can "cooperate" to send crazy messages. For example, the father's value might be that boys don't express feelings, and boys who violate that "rule" are beneath contempt. But the mother might take her son's nondisclosure of feelings as a personal and intolerable rejection.*

   With so many ways to communicate dysfunctionally, what is left? This is a cry we hear often in our classes, sometimes with exasperation, sometimes with despair. One answer is active listening.

---

*See also sarcasm, teasing, mind reading, praising, and approving in the section on Communication Stoppers in Chapter 5.

5

The Magic of Active Listening

THERE IS A KIND OF MAGIC in active listening. I don't understand it, but I see it work.

In conflict situations, I see it reducing defensiveness and hostility, and opening the way to solutions that feel good to all participants. When used by parents toward children, I see active listening enhancing the children's self-esteem. In counseling and therapy, I see it as a powerful tool for reparenting and for elevating self-esteem. In intimate relationships, I see it increasing and deepening feelings of love and trust. In meetings, I see it melting old antagonisms and fixed positions, and reducing boredom and frustration.

What kind of sorcery is this active listening to be so powerful in its effects? Not sorcery at all. Children master it readily if they don't have too many bad communication patterns to unlearn. Some adults find it hard to learn, but others pick it up quickly.

The simplest explanation of active listening's powerful effects is that it clarifies communication and reduces misunderstanding. For example, Billy says, "Dad, are we going to the circus tomorrow?"

Dad replies, "No."

Billy is disappointed and angry. But Billy has learned the value of feedback (as discussed in Chapter 4) to clarify messages. He says, "You mean you don't want to take me even though you promised?"

Dad says, "No, Billy. I mean I'm taking you today, not tomorrow."

By giving feedback, i.e., by saying what message he *received* and asking whether that was the message *sent*, Billy helped to clear up a miscommunication and turned disappointment into joy.

Another example. Seventeen-year-old Cathy asks her father, "What time is it?" If her father listens to the words alone he could answer, "Ten after nine." But if he observes, in addition, that Cathy has been sitting by the phone all evening, that there are tears in her eyes, that her chin is trembling, and that she is dressed up as if to go out, he could feed back these several messages in a way that gives effect to the many levels of Cathy's communication. He says, "I'm seeing a lot of disappointment in you over a call you expected and didn't get. Am I right?" In effect he is saying, "This is my perception of the message you're communicating. Does my perception match the message you're sending?" If his perception is anywhere close to what is real for Cathy, we may expect her tears to brim over in a moment of closeness between her and her father as he signifies, by the simple feedback process, his concern for her and his acceptant knowledge of her. Answering her on a factual level, by giving the time as requested, would have sacrificed the affirmative effects in the relationship that flowed from the father's feedback of the total message as he perceived it.

It's not safe to assume that the message received is the same as the one the Sender intended. Cathy could have responded to her father's feedback with, "No, Daddy, I have a date with Fred tonight, but he's standing by at the hospital with a friend of ours whose mother may be dying, and we're all broken up about it. As soon as anything happens, he'll call." Cathy's response does not mean that her father's feedback was wrong. His feedback was right: he had accurately reflected his perception of the messages he was getting from Cathy, and his feedback served the function for which it was intended, to give Cathy the experience of his perception and to make available to him Cathy's confirmation or correction of what he had fed back.

In these examples, I have tried to illustrate that both the Sender and the Receiver benefit from the Receiver's feedback. The most effective feedback is that which takes account of all the various messages discussed in Chapter 4: words, tone of voice, facial expression, posture, other body signs, silence, context, absence and lateness, and the relationship.

From the feedback process, the following desirable results flow.

1. The Sender feels good about having been attended to.
2. The Sender is enabled to be more effective by either confirming or clarifying his or her message.

3. The Receiver invests in the relationship by sharing his or her perception of the message. (The Receiver's perception, after all, is the product of her or his life experience coming into focus at that moment, and so constitutes a kind of self-revelation, which implies trust in the Sender.)

4. The Receiver gets his or her perception clarified or confirmed, and so is enabled to feel more competent and effective in his or her life, which is a necessary ingredient of self-esteem.

At this point in our classes on *Resolving Family Conflicts So That Everybody Wins,* we begin to see class members shaking their heads and expressing doubt that they can ever learn to be aware of the many levels of communication and to feed them back adequately. Some find it particularly hard to feed back verbally the unspoken feelings that they infer from a Sender's multilevel messages. So let's look at the feedback process in a way to make its simplicity more apparent.

Ten-year-old Tom is talking with his mother.

Tom: I'm never going to that stupid park again.

Mother: When you think about the park, you get pretty angry.

Tom: Yeah, but mostly when I think of that stupid Raymond.

Mother: Raymond's the one you're really angry at.

Tom: Yes, and he's always at the park.

Mother: You'd like to go to the park, but you don't want to have anything to do with Raymond.

Tom: Right. He thinks he's so great.

Mother: You feel kind of put down by him?

Tom: Well, he's always telling me, "Run faster, hit harder, throw farther!" (*Tom's chin trembles.*)

Mother: You feel embarrassed when he points out those things in front of the other kids.

Tom (the tears flow): Why can't I be good at those things like Raymond?

Mother: You feel sad and angry to know that you try so hard, but can't be as good as some of the other kids.

Tom: I feel so stupid.

Mother: When you can't do things Raymond is good at, you just don't feel good at doing anything.

Tom: I'm better at math than he is. And he can't carry a tune.

Mother: You're saying he's good at some things, and you're good at others.

Tom: Everybody's different, I guess.

Mother: I guess so. There are some things I can't do, that I'd like to do, but I just can't.

Tom: Does it make you mad?

Mother: Sometimes. Then I remember that's just the way I am, and my anger goes away.

Tom: You remember that you do other things well.

Mother: That's right.

Mother does active listening at first, then at the end, the roles are reversed and Tom does active listening.

Active Listening Distinguished from Parroting and Paraphrasing

What is active listening? Let's begin by saying what it is not. It is not parroting. Parroting would look something like this:

Tom: I'll never go back to that stupid park again.

Mother: You'll never go back to that stupid park again?

Tom: Especially if Raymond is there.

Mother: Especially if Raymond is there.

My prediction is that Tom will not feel he is being heard very well, even at the outset, and will grow weary and impatient with the encounter after one or two more parroting exchanges, possibly feeling mimicked and put down.

A less mechanical response, one that calls for more involvement by the Receiver, is paraphrasing. Paraphrasing is not active listening. It is, however, an important ingredient of active listening. In paraphrasing, the Receiver feeds back in his own words what he has heard or received from the Sender. For example:

Tom: I'll never go back to that stupid park again.

Mother: Nothing can ever get you back to that stupid park.

Tom: Especially if Raymond is there.

Mother: Raymond is the big reason why you won't go back.

The Receiver makes a bigger investment of herself than was required of her in mere parroting. The additional investment consists of recasting the perceived message into her own words. Although the investment is greater than with parroting, it is still limited to the *content* of the Sender's verbal message. The addition of the Receiver's perception of the Sender transforms paraphrasing into active listening.

To illustrate this difference, let us put the three modes side by side. In parroting:

Tom: I'm never going back to that stupid park again.

Mother: You're never going back to that stupid park again.

In paraphrasing:

Tom: I'm never going back to that stupid park again.

Mother: Nothing can ever get you back to that stupid park.

In active listening:

Tom: I'm never going back to that stupid park again.

Mother: You're so angry that you're just fed up with that park. In parroting, the Receiver gives back the Sender's own words, or virtually so. In paraphrasing, the Receiver gives back what he or she perceives to be the content of the Sender's message, but in the Receiver's own words. In active listening, the Receiver gives back not only a paraphrase of the Sender's message, but also the Receiver's perception of the Sender, specifically the Sender's feelings, attitudes, and perceptions. It is precisely in this feeding back of the Sender's "selfness" as perceived by the Receiver that the magic of active listening lies. The Sender, having risked showing a part of herself or himself, hears in the active listening a message that the Receiver has cared enough to hear the message and to accept both the message and the Sender right where they are. The effect is almost invariably healing, and time after time new energy seems to flow, first into the Sender and then into the Receiver.

Feelings

The principal ingredient of active listening, and the one that most feeds back the Sender's "selfness," is the Receiver's feeding back his or her perception of the Sender's feelings. (For a discussion of what feelings are—and what they are not—see Appendix C.) Feelings seem to be experienced by the owners as part of the self. When I am working with a person in counseling or therapy, if I indicate that I know he or she is, for example, a lawyer, he or she does not ordinarily react as if I had touched on something central to his or her *Self*. The client seems to perceive that I know what he or she *does*, but not that I know something of his or her essence. Similarly, if I know what the client's income is or what kind of car he or she drives, the client seems to experience my knowledge as being about something he or she *has*, rather than of what he or she *is*. The response is quite different, however, when I offer a perception of the client's feelings. The client responds to this kind of offering as though I have touched his or her core. The response may be one of delight or relief at being known, or it may be one of fear, defensiveness, and withdrawal at my getting so close. But it is clear that my feeding back my perception of the client's feelings is experienced by the client as an intimate transaction. And if I can offer my perception of those feelings in an acceptant way, the client seems to experience my offer as healing and as elevating to his or her self-esteem.

So it seems to be worthwhile to look a little more closely at how you can avail yourself of this magic. Let's begin by becoming more clear about the difference between parroting, paraphrasing, and active listening. For that purpose, I want to offer here a series of unrelated statements. Assume that the Sender of each statement is an "important other" in an intimate relationship with you, and to each statement give three responses: first, parroting; second, paraphrasing; and third, active listening. Then we can look at the experience you have had to see how you can use it to build your own active listening skills.

1. I don't know where my next meal is coming from.
2. I'd rather be anywhere but here right now.
3. How I wish I had never said that to him.
4. You tracked mud all over my clean kitchen floor!
5. The kids won't let me play with them.
6. Mary took my skates.
7. You're late for dinner again.
8. The boss called me on the carpet today.
9. You took my ace!

Now let's go back and take a look at your responses. We need not devote much attention to the responses you make in the form of parroting. A parroting response to the first statament would be, "You don't know where your next meal is coming from?" And a parroting response to the second statement would be, "You'd rather be anywhere but here right now?"

When we move from parroting to paraphrasing, however, the variety of responses is infinite, since each Receiver responds in his or her own words, giving his or her understanding of what was heard, and this understanding is shaped by the Receiver's own, unique life experiences. For example, to the first message above, "I don't know where my next meal is coming from," the Receiver could respond with, "You're broke?" or with, "You've come to the end of your resources?" or with, "You have no money left?" and so on. Similarly, to the second statement, "I'd rather be anywhere but here," the Receiver could respond with, "This place is no good for you?" or "Of all the places you might be, this is last on your preference list?" and so on. These responses show that the Receiver is giving more than perfunctory attention to the Sender's message; the Receiver is investing himself or herself in the transaction, saying in effect, "I'm paying attention to your message. It has meaning for me. I want to give you that meaning in my own words, so that you can decide for yourself whether the meaning I get is the meaning you intend."

But the Receiver can invest even more, with important and enriching consequences in the relationship. This further investment is an active-listening response. In this response the Receiver feeds back his or her own paraphrase of the message received, plus something more. That something more is (1) the Receiver's perception of the Sender's feeling state (i.e., not only the content of the message sent by the Sender, but also the essence of the Sender in sending the message) and (2) an attitude of acceptance, not necessarily agreement or approval, but what Carl Rogers calls "unconditional positive regard." For example, to the first statement, "I don't know where my next meal is coming from," an active-listening response could be, "You're broke and feeling anxious about the future," or, "It must be scary to face starvation," or, "When you talk about being unable even to buy food, I hear despair in your voice," and so on. Similarly, to the second statement, "I'd rather be anywhere but here," an active-listening response could be, "It sounds as though you attach a lot of negative feelings to this place," or, "The way you say that sounds like wanting to run away," or, "You must be feeling trapped at having to be here," and so on. Each of these examples contains more than paraphrasing. The added element is the Receiver's acceptant perception of the Sender's feelings, which were either contained in the verbal message or sent simultaneously as nonverbal communications. As with paraphrasing, the number and variety of active-listening responses is infinite. The same Receiver can respond to the same message in a variety of ways, depending on his or her own feeling state at the moment, the context, and an endless variety of other influences. Moreover, each Receiver will respond uniquely, because the Receiver's response is based on his or her own unique life experience up to that moment.

Skilled active listeners account for the keenness of their perceptions in a variety of ways: logical inference, intuition, empathy born of similar experience. Whatever the reasons, active listening seems to sharpen the active listener's sensitivity to others, and this sensitivity makes active listening more effective.

We have now been introduced to active listening. Why have we examined it in such detail? For two reasons. First, the responses given in active listening tend to enhance the Sender's self-esteem. It is thus a tool for "people making," particularly (but not exclusively) when active listening is used with children. With higher self-esteem, the Sender in return can invest more in the relationship and contribute more to it, with consequent elevation of the Receiver's self-esteem and good feeling. Second, active listening reduces tension in relationships, diminishes defensiveness, and clarifies messages, so that conflicts in relationships maybe resolved in ways that strengthen and enrich the relationship.

With all these advantages, why isn't active listening used by more people more of the time? The big answer—even though it is not an answer at all—seems to be, simply, that active listening is unfamiliar. We have been so conditioned to using other ways that we stick to those ways despite repeated and continuing evidence that they don't work. Let's take a look now at some of the familiar ways we use, so that we can recognize them and avoid them in situations in which active listening would be much more effective.

Communication Stoppers

In our class, we hand out a mimeographed list of communication stoppers, like that below, and watch as the class members read the list. Typically, there are shamefaced groans and embarrassed laughter as the class members identify their own behaviors on the list. When they have read to the end, there is much head shaking, and then somebody asks, "What's left? If we can't use these responses, what *can* we use?"

In fact, they *can* and do use these responses, and that fact is largely responsible for their enrolling in our class. They come to the class realizing that the responses they have been using in their families and other relationships have not been working effectively. They come to the class in search of more effective ways to bring about more rewarding relationships. For many of them, the list of communication stoppers is the first indication they have had that their habitual ways of responding have been poisoning their relationships. So when they ask, "What else is there?" we recognize the question as a cry from the heart, and as an exciting first step in their progress toward finding better ways.

Here is a list of communication stoppers. These are common forms of response to children, employees, intimates, and others which deny validity to the feelings and self-esteem, and thus to the very essence, of the person addressed.

Solution Messages

First there are the *solution messages,* most of which have a put-down effect.

1. Directing, ordering, commanding (e.g., "Stop crying," "Try harder," "You must...") typically produce fright, defensiveness, resistance, and resentment. These forms teach authoritarianism and disqualify feelings. At one extreme they may arouse retaliation, revenge, or rebellion. At the other, they may contribute to the formation of a meek, fearful, placating personality.

2. Threatening, warning, punishing (e.g., "If you do, you'll be grounded (fired)"; "You'd better...") produce resentment, fear, anger, and resistance, invite testing or sabotage, and teach authoritarianism. This approach may arouse rebellion, revenge, or retaliation, or it may result in passivity, despair, or manipulation.

3. Preaching, moralizing (e.g., "Nice girls don't do that"; "You should..."") tend to induce guilt, reduce self-esteem, shift the base of moral or ethical authority from a well-developed, internal, adult capacity for judgment to an other-directed reliance on what people "out there" will think, or, at the other extreme, may build resistance to socially accepted values.

4. Persuading, arguing, lecturing (e.g., "The fact is...," "When you're older, you'll realize...") emphasize the persuader's or lecturer's "rightness," may habituate the other person to his or her "wrongness," invite counterarguments, increase defensiveness, reduce openness, and invalidate feelings.

5. Advising, recommending (e.g., "What you should do is...," "Why don't you...") imply superiority, deprive the Receiver of the esteem-building experience of solving his or her own problem, may encourage dependency, and invite a "yes but" game.

Put-Down Messages

The *put-down messages* as such don't even propose a solution.

6. Criticizing, name-calling, chararacterizing, blaming (e.g., "You fouled up our plan," "You never...," "You always...," "Liar," "Thief," "You're a typical lawyer") lower self-esteem, induce guilt feelings, reduce openness, arouse resentment and retaliation at one extreme, or may lead to acceptance of and surrender to the negative judgment at the other extreme.

7. Sarcasm, teasing (e.g., "So the world is all wrong and you're all right") arouse feelings of rejection, resentment, hostility, and possibly the frustration of being unable to discern the real message hidden by the indirect one. This is a crazy-making device.

8. Diagnosing, psychoanalyzing, mind reading (e.g., "You're just saying that because you're overtired"; "It's just a phase you're going through"; "You're just hostile to men") are generally experienced as threatening to privacy and as rejecting one's self-perception, arousing anger and defensiveness at one extreme, or possibly undermining basic self-trust and self-perception at the other. This is another "crazy-making" response.

Cop-Out Messages

The *cop-out messages* are ones that take attention away from the present situation.

9. Withdrawing, Diverting (e.g., "I won't discuss it any further"; "Not now") communicate a lack of respect for the other and possibly anxiety in the Sender. The "silent treatment" often has, in addition, a punishing effect. Unresolved transactions typically lead to storing up grievances and distorting later transactions.

10. Cross-examining, interrogating, fact-finding (e.g., "You must have done something to bring it about"; "Are you sure you're telling the truth?") ignore the other person's feelings, may communicate mistrust, and divert attention to what happened there and then, instead of to the feelings, purposes, attitudes, and intentions present here and now between the interrogator and his or her victim.

Pseudo-Supportive Messages

The *supposedly supportive messages* are ones that instead have negative effects.

11. Praising, approving (e.g., 'That's a good job"; "You drew a pretty house") are usually well-intended (when they are not manipulative), but they imply that the Sender can judge the other's performance, and they raise the possibility that the next performance may be disapproved, perhaps only by failure to express approval. The relationship created is that of judge/supplicant. One negative effect of this kind of communication stopper is to dry up creativity. For example, the principal value to a small child in making a new water-color painting may be in the colors or shapes or strokes, or perhaps even the mere fact that he or she has undertaken the effort at all. For the parent to praise the effort as "a nice house" or to fact-find the effort with "What is it?" denies the child any reward for his or her own creativity, and values the result of the child's effort only for what it looks like or signifies to the parent. These messages can weaken self-confidence and independent judgment.

12. Reassuring, consoling, excusing, sympathizing (e.g., "It will feel better in the morning"; "I'm sure he doesn't dislike you as much as you think") fail to express understanding of and empathy for the very pain these messages are intended to reduce. With very young children, if the reassurance proves overly optimistic, trust may be reduced. The Sender's basic purpose in sending this kind of reassurance is probably to reduce the Sender's own anxiety in the presence of the Receiver's pain. The message received may be "Don't have negative feelings—and don't be aware of them if you have them."

13. *Me Too messages* (e.g., "I have that trouble too"; "I can identify with that because . . ."; "I know exactly how you feel") are usually intended to express identity with and understanding of the other person, but have the effect of diverting attention from that person to the intervenor.

This is my list of communication stoppers. You may be able to draw others from your own experience. For me the grave and sometimes astonishing part of this list is how habitually most of us use such ways of responding without thinking how damaging they are, both to the relationship and to the self-esteem of the recipient.

This brings us back to the question, if these thirteen ways of responding are undesirable, ineffective and even damaging, what is left? What can we use? Let's try active listening.

6

When to Use Active Listening

IN THIS CHAPTER I want to describe some powerful effects of active listening and take a closer look at how to use it most effectively—and when not to use it.   Imagine that some person you care about comes to you with strong feelings about a situation in which you're not involved. It could be your young son pitching his heart out for his little league team and allowing twenty earned runs in the first inning. It could be your daughter being stood up for a date. It could be your husband having been threatened with the loss of a job he very much wants. It could be your wife feeling anxious about the impression she is about to make on somebody important to you. Or it could be an employee or subordinate of yours in a rage or tears over some disturbing incident at home. In each of these situations, the Sender has a problem and you have an opportunity to respond. You could use the Communication Stoppers listed in Chapter 5 and get the negative effects described there. Or you could use active listening.

Here let me indicate the power of active listening when the Sender has a problem and you are the Receiver.

When Sender Has a Problem

Imagine a young bride who is about to meet her husband's employer for the first time.

75

Sue: Is this dress okay? Is this the sort of thing your boss would like?

Joe: You sound nervous, anxious, wanting to make a good impression on him, but unsure how to do it.

Sue: I'm feeling awfully unsure.

Joe: It's important to you that he approve of you?

Sue: It is important. What if I spill the gravy or say the wrong thing?

Joe: You're afraid that if you do anything wrong, he'll disapprove of you?

Sue: Yes. I guess if he were going to judge me on such superficial tests, I wouldn't have to respect him all that much, would I?

Joe: So you're a little more ready now to form your own judgment of yourself and not leave it all to him.

Sue: Yes. I like this dress. I'll wear it.

On the surface, Sue's opening statement asks for a judgment about the appropriateness of the dress and about the employer's taste and preference. Joe could have answered with, "The dress is okay, dear. I'm sure he'll like it." But in my experience, this kind of reassurance (being a Communication Stopper, type 12) does not reassure. It is more likely to be perceived by Sue as expressing a wish by Joe that she would not have or express anxious feelings. This is a form of rejection, which undermines self-esteem and increases anxiety. Had she derived comfort from Joe's reassurance, it would have been a kind of dependent band-aid job, setting up Joe as the source of her strength.

Instead of responding to the *content* of Sue's message, Joe correctly perceives her question as a cry of pain and responds on that more intimate level. Instead of following Sue's verbal message, which is in the form of a request for information, Joe tunes in on the basic self in Sue's message, the feelings and emotions implicit in her communication. His tone and manner, supportive and acceptant, and his active listening convey the unstated message, "I'm attuned to the person you are, to the feelings you have. I care about the anxiety you suffer, and I trust you to have the strength to handle your feelings in the supportive environment I provide." This leaves it open for Sue to turn her attention from her dress and the boss's preference—in terms of which she will never find resolution—to her feelings and her power and competence. Here I have a sense that Sue's change of perception and direction is solid and dependable, because she came to it on her own, using her own experience and her own self-perception.

So part of the power of active listening is that it validates the Sender, enhances her self-esteem, and elevates her sense of competence and power in her world.

Another result of active listening is to build feelings of closeness and intimacy between Sender and Receiver. If Joe and Sue had talked about her dress and the boss's preferences, they would not have been talking about Joe and Sue. But when Joe feeds back the Sue he perceives in her message, and he does this attentively, acceptantly, supportively, they are, in a way, entering into each other intimately, getting to know each other more fully and deeply, and experiencing safety with each other.

Let us take another example. You, at age ten, have lost your dog, Bowzer. Your parent uses active listening.

You: (crying).
Parent (compassionately): Oh, such tears!
You: My dog just died.
Parent: Oh, how that must hurt you!
You: I loved him better than anybody in the whole world.
Parent: The way you feel now, nobody can take his place.
You: What am I going to do?
Parent: You want to do something for the pain in you, but you can't think what that could be?
You: We used to have such fun.
Parent: So one thing you can do is think of the happy times.
You: We did have happy times.
Parent: The way I see you now, those memories are very dear to you.
You: Yes.
Parent: Your tears have stopped for now.
You: Yes.
Parent: Sadness and happy memories together.
You: Yes.

As with Joe and Sue, the actively listening parent seeks out the You in your messages, validates you as you are, sends you verbal and nonverbal messages of support and acceptance, and communicates that feelings are all right, that they do not get out of hand, and that you are to be trusted to handle whatever is real in you. Closeness, intimacy, trust, and love are the by-products of this transaction.

When Sender Is Ready

Active listening is not always appropriate. For example, if a member of your family runs into the room yelling, "Quick, where's the fire extinguisher?" it is probably not appropriate to respond with, "I can see that you are afraid. Would you like to tell me about it?" There is little doubt that the Sender has a problem, but it's the kind of problem that calls for information or action as the response.

Not all messages in the form of a question, however, call for information or action. If your lover asks you, "Do you have all your evenings committed next week?" he or she may, in reality, be expressing feelings of neglect, rejection, or even mistrust, suspicion, or jealousy. If one of your children asks, "Why do I have to go to school?" he or she probably does not want reasons; the message, more likely, is an expression of discontent. In either situation, active listening is appropriate, as it was appropriate betwen Sue and Joe, even though her message was in the form of a question.

Receiver's Sense of Sender's Readiness (Intuition)

Sometimes I hear an exasperated client ask, "Well, how am I supposed to know when a question is or is not a question?" I wish I had a foolproof answer; I can't always tell. What I keep on learning to do is to watch and listen for more than the verbal message. I rely more and more on the sense I get of the person sending the message. I like to call this sense intuition, but I meet a lot of people who think they don't have intuition; some of them even seem to think that intuition is like extrasensory perception, or a supernatural connection to a source of information not available to them. In any event, that's not what I mean. When I say intuition, I am talking about our ability to make use of two sources of information that I think nearly everybody has. One is a sensitivity to minimal clues, e.g., tone of voice, facial expression, body posture, a pause, a slip of the tongue, an averted glance, a blush, a tightening of muscles, the appearance of tears. This sensitivity can be sharpened.

The other source of information is an awareness of my internal process. Stored away in my memory bank is the accumulated product of my experience. Much of that experience is not available to me as direct memory of incidents and events, but the products of that experience— attitudes, conclusions, reflex responses, prejudices, automatic survival reactions, etc.—are available to me if I allow myself to be aware of them and to trust them.

When I talk about trusting my internal process—my "body"—I am aware that it can betray me. Stored away with the good stuff are prejudices, old guilt tapes, and other distortions in my perceptions. It is important to me to bring those distortions into awareness and to work them through, so that they will not corrupt my view of present realities. Meanwhile, I can trust my body more and more as an important source of information, because it contains data that would not be available to me if I limited myself to information that I could document with "good reasons." How many times have I said to myself ruefully, "If I had only trusted my better judgment!" Most of the times when I didn't trust my "better judgment," I had limited myself to decisions for which I could come up with "good reasons," meaning reasons in awareness. But I had neglected my storehouse of reasons no longer in awareness. This accumulation of gut wisdom, born of experience but no longer in awareness in the form of "reasons," is part of what I call intuition.

If I draw fully on those two parts of my intuitive process, I have a lot of information available to use in my transactions with important others in my life. I grow more sensitive to them, more aware of them, more empathic toward them, and consequently more dear to them and more trusted by them.

And it is easier, then, for me to distinguish their questions that are simple requests for action or information from those that are hidden statements of feelings and for which active listening would be appropriate and productive.

Sender Acknowledges Existence of a Discussable Problem

It isn't enough for the Sender to have a problem and the Receiver to perceive the Sender's problem. No matter how grave the problem the Sender may have, active listening is not appropriate unless the sender (a) is aware that he or she has a problem and (b) is willing to talk about it.

For example, if you smoke cigarettes to excess and are thus injuring your health, but have decided to continue smoking, regardless of the effects on your health, you will probably not see yourself as having the kind of problem for which you would regard active listening as appropriate. Similarly, a teenager's parents may see his or her pattern of social nonconformity as indicating that the teenager has a problem, but attempts at active listening will probably be fruitless until the teenager also sees his or her behavior as evidence of (or as constituting) a problem.

Moreover, the problem is a problem only to the extent that the Sender defines it as a problem. For example, if an employee complains of being discriminated against by his or her employer, the Receiver may perceive that the Sender's own behavior is provoking the problem. Active listening to that "problem," however, is not appropriate and may be counterproductive.*

The problem is generally an experience in which the Sender experiences pain, frustration, or some other negative feeling. The Sender may be experiencing a lack of power or competence to cope with the

---

*As I said earlier, we need not reserve active listening only for problems. It is equally appropriate when the Sender wants to share positive feelings. I emphasize "problem" feelings and emotions here because I have observed that the sharing of positive feelings rarely presents problems in a relationship; it's in the sharing of negative feelings that the difficulties arise and that the major opportunities for active listening present themselves.

situation in his or her life, or may be suffering from the behavior of another person which the Sender perceives to be a problem for him or her. In either situation, active listening is appropriate, given that the Sender perceives the situation to be a problem and is ready to share it with this particular Receiver.

There is a third situation in which active listening is appropriate: when your behavior is a problem to me, or my behavior is a problem to you, i.e., when the Receiver's own behavior is a problem to the Sender. In that situation, however, the active listening is used as part of the techniques of conflict resolution and problem solving discussed in later chapters.

Sender Is Willing for Receiver to Listen Actively

If the previously discussed tests for the appropriateness of active listening have been met—the Sender acknowledges that there is a problem, and is ready to share it—there remains another test: the Sender must be willing to have the Receiver participate as an active listener. For example, my sexual relationship with my lover may be a problem to me, and I may be well aware that it is a problem. I may even be eager to discuss it with somebody. But I may not want to share that problem with my employer, even if my worry about it affects my performance at work. If my employer, even with the best of intentions, tries to serve as active listener to my problem, his efforts are likely to be met with reluctance, probably with refusal or dissimulation, and possibly with resentment and hostility.

When Receiver is Empathic and Undistracted

When you engage in active listening, you are making a partial but important gift of yourself to the Sender. The gift consists of your opening and revealing yourself to the Sender, which also implies trust. And giving trust to another is a risk.

The active listener's implied message is, "This is the message I am getting from you. In revealing what message I am getting, I am really disclosing my own perceptions. Since my perceptions are based on my experience, revealing my perceptions is revealing something about me. In disclosing myself to you, I render myself vulnerable to your using this disclosure about me in either benign or hurtful ways. I choose this risk because I care enough about you to trust you not to use my disclosures in hurtful ways. I care enough about my relationship with you to want to strengthen it by taking this risk."

For me to make that kind of investment in another person as an active listener requires two conditions: (1) I feel empathic toward the Sender at this moment; and (2) I am free from distractions and diversions that would get in the way of focusing on the Sender.

Empathy

Students in our classes on active listening report great difficulty in actually experiencing the Sender's emotional state. Evidently most of us are conditioned to tune in on "what happened" and "how did it happen" and what to do. We're not conditioned to step inside this Sender's skin, so to speak, and really to identify with and take on the Sender's own set of feelings, attitudes, and perceptions.

To help build this capacity for empathy, we do a lot of role playing in our classes. (We do this not in the negative sense of taking a stereotypical role, but in the positive sense of taking on a character or personality so thoroughly that the actor virtually becomes the character portrayed.) If, for example, a husband and wife are working on a conflict between themselves, we sometimes suggest that the wife take the role of the husband and the husband the role of the wife, and that they engage in the same conflict from these reversed postures. Often the first thing we observe is that they feel utterly unable to get into the partner's role. Sometimes it is a sharp revelation to one or both of them that, after living with the same person for many years in an intimate relationship, they do not really know inside themselves what it feels like to be that partner. As one woman cried, on realizing this limitation, "I've been living with a stranger!" But with time, with more attention to the other party in the relationship, and with more experience in trying to take that partner's role in real situations, the capacity for empathy flowers.

Carl Rogers' description of empathy in the counselor applies also to empathy in any human relationship, and to the active listener's attitude or set: "It is the counselor's function to assume, insofar as he is able, the internal frame of reference of the client, to perceive the world as the client sees it, to perceive the client himself as he is seen by himself, to lay aside all perceptions from the external frame of reference while doing so, and to communicate something of this empathic understanding to the client." (1965, p. 29). In another formulation on the same page, Rogers quotes Nathaniel J. Raskin: The "counselor participation becomes an active experiencing with the client of the feelings to which he gives expression, the counselor makes a maximum effort to get under the skin of the person with whom he is communicating, he tries to get *within* and to live the attitudes expressed instead of observing them, to catch every nuance of their changing nature; in a word, to absorb himself completely in the attitudes of the other."

These descriptions of empathy appear to be formidable and are sometimes disheartening. I want to emphasize, however, that children reared in homes in which active listening and empathic attitudes are regular parts of the environment have hardly any difficulty with either empathy or active listening, and adults who enter optimistically into the process of unlearning their old conditioning pick up these new ways sometimes with astonishing rapidity. I myself was one of the late-comers to empathy and active listening, having been reared and trained in the tradition of facts and reason, not feelings. I will not pretend that the switchover was easy, and it would be arrogant to assert that I have mastered it. But the testimony of my family, and of the staff at the Center where I work, is that I have acquired a reasonable facility with empathy and active listening. That I have done so demonstrates that these attitudes and skills can be acquired even relatively late in life; I am approaching age 67 as I write this, and was about 57 years old when I first encountered active listening.

I've given myself one gift concerned with active listening and empathy that might be valuable for you to give yourself. I've given myself permission to be much less than totally empathic, and to be awkward and sometimes ineffective in my use of active listening. Armed with this permission, I have often achieved good results from trying active listening in situations where I would not even have tried it had I set myself a goal of perfection. The risk I take in going ahead in the face of self-doubt seems in itself to be appreciated and to have positive effects.

One of the key ingredients in empathy is intuition. As I sharpen my sensitivity to minimal clues, and as I learn more and more to "trust my body" as a source of wisdom, judgment, and inference born of the accumulation of my life's experience, I find myself more and more able to put myself into the other person's framework as described by Rogers and Raskin. Sometimes I do this so completely that I shed my own tears in resonance to those of the client—and similarly with other emotions.

Relative Freedom from Distraction

If you are at all like me, you are not going to empathize very effectively if you have an awful headache or if you are late for an important appointment. To expect to give anyone an empathic hearing under those circumstances would merely impose foolishly unrealistic expectations on yourself. Accept yourself as you know yourself to be; do not lay expectations of perfection on yourself that your body will work against. Trust your body's wisdom.

Here are some of the common distractions that I see people trying unsuccessfully to ignore.

Bodily distractions. These include headache, stomachache, toothache, other nagging pains, need to urinate or defecate, nausea, hunger, tension, stress, and nervousness.

Conflicting demands on time and attention. Lateness for an appointment or deadline, the demands of children or other family members, distracting noises or visual interruptions; these are a few of the conflicting demands.

Distractions from the past. I can best illustrate this category of distraction with examples. If my wife expresses fear of physical disability due to arthritis, I may have difficulty focusing on her problem if I grew up with my own fears resulting from my mother's physical disability when I was very young. The present situation triggers in me a distracting emotional set established by incidents in my past. The result is that I am distracted, at least initially, from attending as empathically as I would like to. Similarly, Marco grew up in a large, competitive family in which he learned to expect to have to fight bitterly just to survive. It may be difficult for him to listen empathically to a co-worker or a family member expressing a request that he exhibit more trust and tenderness, or for him to hear the pain and yearning expressed by the other.

Another kind of distraction from the past may be feelings and attitudes resulting from the Receiver's experience with this particular Sender. If Jill says, "I never seem to be able to do anything right," her father might be expected to respond with compassion and empathy. If, however, he has heard the same declaration many times over and has experienced it as a device to manipulate him on several occasions in the past, he may be inclined to take a skeptical and self-protective stance that would deflect him, at least initially, from attending empathically to Jill's expression of pain.

I do not mean that *any* distraction makes active listening impossible. I mean merely that distractions make empathic listening more difficult, and that this difficulty increases as the gravity and urgency of the distraction increase. An attempt to give empathic listening in the face of a severe distraction may fail. What works for me is to be aware that I am suffering from a distraction, and to decide whether that distraction is severe enough to prevent me from giving the kind of empathic attention that I want to give. If it is, I want to give my distraction respectful attention, until it has abated sufficiently to allow me to give the other the attention that I want to give. Often in this situation, I reveal my distraction to the Sender.

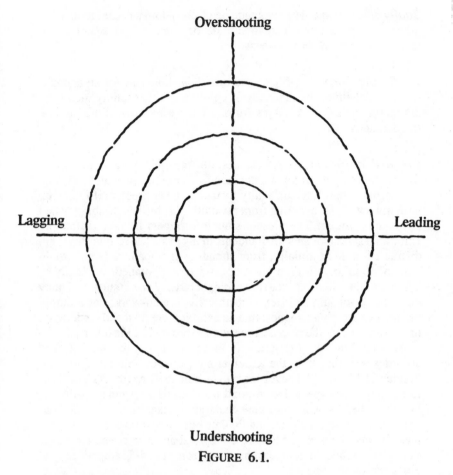

FIGURE 6.1.

Active Listening on Target

Active listening works best as a mover and healer when the Receiver's feedback reflects exactly where the Sender is, neither lagging nor leading, neither overshooting nor undershooting (see Figure 6.1). Let's look first at the difference between lagging and on-target active listening.

Lagging

Daughter: Mother, I'm a grown woman now with a husband and children of my own.

Mother (active listening): And you're pretty angry at me.

Daughter: Yes, I am angry. You keep giving me advice as if I were eight years old.

Mother: And you don't like that.

Daughter: No, I don't. I'd like you to respect my ability to make my own judgments.

Mother: And you see me interfering with that.

Daughter: Well, not all the time, but sometimes.

Mother: Yes.

Daughter: And to be fair to you, you don't really do it often.

Mother: But you'd like me to keep my advice to myself.

In this dialog I have tried to illustrate a desirable and common result of active listening. The daughter discloses that she experiences her mother's behavior as a problem and has some strong feelings about it. The mother indicates by her nondefensive responses that she feels empathy and concern for her daughter's feelings. In the course of the dialog, the daughter's anger subsides, and she is able to move away from the blanket condemnation implied by her first statement to a more and more conciliatory and friendly set of responses ("not all the time . . . you don't really do it often"). Instead of going with this movement, however, the mother returns to the daughter's earlier, more hostile statement, ignoring the movement that has apparently taken place in the dialog and in the daughter's feelings. This return to an earlier statement or feeling, ignoring the movement that may have taken place since then, is called lagging.

Leading

Leading is the opposite of lagging. In leading, the active listener anticipates the direction in which the Sender seems to be going before the Sender is ready. For example:

Minnie: I'm afraid my marriage is in trouble.

Jake: You seem to be hurting a lot.

Minnie: I really am. I just don't know what to do.

Jake: Feeling confused and helpless.

Minnie: Yes, I am. Sometimes it seems as though everything I try is wrong.

Jake: And divorce is the only answer.

In this dialog the sudden mention of divorce seems to me to be premature and startling. My feeling for the situation is that Minnie is at the stage of looking at her pain and helplessness and inability to master the situation, and has not yet moved to the stage of looking at her options or directions. It may be that she will bring the conversation around to the subject of divorce—may even do so just one or two statements later—but that she has not yet reached that point in this dialog. Jake, in raising the subject of divorce, is doing more than reflecting back his perception of Minnie's statements, more than listening actively to where she is. Minnie is likely to feel that the subject is startling and instrusive, and if a subject raised by Jake is at all scary to her, it may be hard for her to return to an examination of her problem.

Undershooting

Carol: I'm so mad I could chew nails.
Bob: You're a little upset.
Undershooting is active listening that fails to reflect accurately the true intensity and extent of the Sender's message. The Sender is likely to feel not very well-heard.

Overshooting

Salesman: Boss, I think somebody else on our staff would be more effective with this customer than I am.
Boss: You feel totally inadequate to deal with this customer.
Overshooting is the opposite of undershooting. In overshooting, the active listener overstates the intensity or extent of the Sender's message.

Movement in Active Listening

The preceding discussion of on-target and off-target active listening indicates that active listening at its most effective facilitates change and movement in the feelings of the Sender. When the Receiver gives effective active listening, the most immediate result is the Sender's perception that he or she is being heard, which itself gives a sense of relief from the discomfort that the Sender is expressing.

In addition to this sense of relief, the Sender may experience a reduction in any self-condemnation that may be present. Such "beating yourself up" is sometimes expressed in phrases like, "What is the matter with me," "Things like this always happen to me," or "I just hate myself for doing that." Under the nurturance of the Receiver's empathic acceptance, the Sender can feel more acceptant of himself or herself, and consequently more ready to examine his or her own motives, feelings, and perceptions, and to consider changes in them and in his or her behaviors.

A third consequence of effective active listening is something I can describe adequately only as a kind of love. Time after time, when I work with families or couples or groups, and one person gives another a gift of empathic listening and feedback, I see a quality of love emerge. Whether you call it love or something else, the effective active listener somehow brings about a sense of connection laced with gratitude and relief, and warmed with feelings of trust that brighten the Sender's self-image and sense of competence and belonging; as a result, Sender and Receiver come to feel far more joined together and far safer with each other than they had before the Sender began his or her message.

In *Client Centered Therapy*, a client describes the experience of being heard and valued by the counselor:

"My first reaction to you, I think, was one of surprise at your sensitivity and awareness of what and how I was feeling, even when I expressed it very inarticulately or not at all. I knew you were quick and sensitive, but I didn't think anyone could be *that* understanding.

"Then I began to get the feeling that not only were you sensitive to and understanding of my feelings, but you also *cared* and cared very much."

Movement can take place with active listening:

Client: I'm thinking of leaving my family.

Counselor: As you see it, you just can't work things out?

Client: Right. They all see me as a kind of money tree, and that's about all.

Counselor: The way you see it, they don't value you very much for yourself alone.

Client: That's right. Sometimes I wonder if they even know I'm there, except when they want another handout.

Counselor: You'd like them to value you for more than mere handouts.

Client: I sure would. Other people seem to know that but my family never does.

Counselor: As you see it, you never get anything but demands from your family.

Client: Well, I wouldn't say never—almost never.

Counselor: Sometimes you do get some of the recognition you'd like.

Client: Well, yes, but not much.

Counselor: You'd like it to be a lot more.

Client: I sure would. Instead, all I get is bitching about how much time I put in at work.

Counselor: You feel their pressure to be with them more.

Client: Well, I can't spend more time at home and still give them everything they want.

Counselor: You feel kind of squeezed.

Client: I sure do, and I'm fed up.

Counselor: Sounds like a determination to put a stop to the squeezing, to consider other options.

Client: Right. And one of them is simply to get out of that family.

Counselor: You see that as one of a number of options.

Client: Yes, and another one is to learn to say *no* a lot more than I do.

Counselor: So you have the power to change the situation even if you remain with the family.

Client: Yes, I have. And I guess I have more power over what I do, don't I?

Counselor: You're saying that you can be more effective by modifying your own behavior than by trying to get them to change?

Client: That's the way it looks, and one change I can make is just to let them know what my limits are.

Counselor: From your body stance I would guess that you feel good about that option.

Client: Yes, I do. I don't have to be a doormat; I can tell them what I want.

Counselor: A lot of power in that.

Client: And I can still hear what they want without having to say *yes* all the time.

Counselor: You seem to be looking now at a more workable kind of family life.

Client: And I think we can get that.

Notice that the counselor has not given advice or suggested the direction of the client's change. He has simply paraphrased the client's statements and added his perception of the client's feelings. In that environment the client has seen and followed his own opportunities for change. In the client's initial statement only one option is seen, fleeing from an intolerable situation that the client thinks himself powerless to change. At the end the client appears to be aware of a number of options and of his power to get what he wants.

Active Listener's Power

The active listener is not just a mirror. In fact, the active listener is an active participant in many ways, and has much power to shape the direction of the transaction. At its most elementary level, the active listener's power is the power to give relief to the Sender just by giving empathic focus and feedback, and so to create a sense of competence and a kind of love.

Another element of the active listener's power to shape the transaction lies in the judgments that the Receiver necessarily makes in deciding which part of the Sender's message to feed back. For example, your fourth-grader comes home from school saying, "That teacher is stupid. She tells us exactly how to do our artwork, as though

we don't have any brains. But I don't do it." Some of the many possible active-listening responses to the above statement are:
— "You seem to be really angry at your teacher."
— "You don't have much respect for her teaching methods."
— "You'd like the teacher to show a lot more respect for your creativity."
— "You feel a lot of power to do things your own way."
— "It's frustrating when the teacher gets in the way of your expressing yourself."

It is apparent that the response chosen by the active listener influences the Sender's next message. In the preceding example, one active-listening response emphasizes the Sender's frustration, another the Sender's anger, another the Sender's power; one centers on the Sender's feeling toward the teacher, another on feelings toward the project, another on feeling toward the Sender's own creativity. Thus even a well-intentioned active listener can keep the Sender from moving, rather than facilitate movement. If the Receiver were to emphasize the teacher's faults and the Sender's frustration, the fourth-grader might continue emphasizing the hopelessness and frustration of the situation until one or both of them become exhausted by the fruitlessness of the transaction or turned off by the whining.

Active-listening responses that acknowledge the Sender's creativity and power are in my judgment more likely to produce some change and to result in a feeling of resolution or closure. Some of the messages I listen for and respond to in active listening are as follows:

Hope. Very often families and couples are so caught up in their pain that they have lost touch with feelings of hope that might motivate them in their efforts to heal wounds and ruptures in their relationships. Kevin and Laura express despair over their angry fighting. When I feed back to them the despair expressed in their words, but also the hope implied by their coming to me for counseling, I see them begin moving toward exploration of the factors that hold them together, along with those they had been emphasizing as keeping them apart.

Power. Most fights, in my perception, are screaming matches, in which the metamessage sent by each is, "Listen to me; hear me." The frustration of not being heard in a significant relationship is so great that it may, and often does, erupt in anger and sometimes violence. The human organism seems to need some way to reassert power when it is frustrated by inability to attain what it wants or needs. On this assumption, I will be more effective as an active listener if I try to pick up and feed back any sense of power that the Sender has and can validly exploit. The fourth-grader mentioned above has a sense of his power to ignore the teacher's command, and so to exercise some control in his life. The client in an earlier example is helped to recognize that he is not utterly powerless in his family, but has the power to modify his own behavior to get more of what he wants.

Choice. One of the powers an active listener can emphasize is the power of choice. If a client says to me, "I seem to be stuck in this job," I feed back not only the verbal message but also the context; my feedback responses would be something like, "For now, choosing to stay on that job seems to you to be preferable to all the other things you might choose to do at this time." If he answers, "I have to stay on that job; I have no choice," I'm likely to respond with, "The option of leaving the job seems to you like a bad choice at this time." This shift of emphasis, from the powerlessness to the power of choice, usually arouses or at least encourages in the Sender a renewed sense of competence and power in her or his life, and enhances his or her self-esteem and confidence.

Love messages. Couples and families in conflict tend to ignore love messages tucked away in what they say and do to one another.

Jean says to Samuel, "Your lovemaking is too rough. I keep asking you for tenderness and love, and all you give me is violent sex."

Samuel responds, "I don't seem to be able to do anything to please you," or "You seem to like it when I do it, but then you hit me with it afterward."

At this point I may intervene with, "I heard Jean sending a love message. I heard her say in effect that she thinks about making love with you, and about how it could be made better for her." Similarly, if a teenager complains that her parent is unduly restrictive, and worries about her late hours too much, I may comment to the parent that he or she seems not to be getting across to the teenager the love that underlies the worry. Alert active listeners can build skill in picking up and expressly verbalizing these hidden love messages, and thus strongly influencing the course of a dialog.

Discrepant or inconsistent messages. Sometimes a client says to me, "I don't even want to be here." My feedback to him or her may be something like, "Your words say that you don't want to be here, but your behavior says that you choose to be here." This kind of feedback encourages the Sender to look at inconsistencies in his or her messages, and possibly at conflict in motivations and purposes, and may facilitate dramatic new perceptions or, at least, significant changes in the direction of the feelings in the dialog. Similarly, a parent may say to a ten-year-old, "You're not big enough to take responsibility for a ten-speed bicycle," but later may say to the same child, "You're old enough to take responsibility for your tools much better than you've been doing." If the child is alert to the active-listening possibilities presented by this discrepancy (and many ten-year-olds are adept at this), he or she could feed back this inconsistency and possibly bring about in the parent a shift in both perception and behavior on this particular issue.

Always or never messages. The words *always* and *never* are often heard in the encounters of dysfunctional families. In such families it is not unusual to hear one member say to another, "You never listen to me," or "You're always on my back." Virginia Satir, author of *Conjoint Family Therapy,* feeds these messages back so literally that the Sender is usually quick to back off from the absolute, blanket nature of his statement. If a twelve-year-old complains, "I never get a chance to choose what we watch on television," the active-listening response might be, "there is never, ever a time in your family when you get a chance to choose the television program. It is always without exception someone else who chooses what the family watches." Expectedly the Sender's response is usually something like, "Well, sometimes I get a chance to choose, but . . ." In time such a Sender can be sensitized by this kind of feedback to the difference between what he or she knows to be true in his or her world and what he or she presents as true in the present emotional state. This new sensitivity can, and usualy does, result in shifts in perception and direction, as well as in the Sender's sense of power and self-esteem.

Self-blame. Put-downs of oneself are common. You have probably many times heard such phrases as, "I hate myself for doing that," or "That was so stupid of me," or "I just can't seem to do anything right." An active listener can legitimately feed back simply the discouragement or impatience or anger or frustration expressed by such statements, but some other active-listening responses are better at producing movement in a direction the Sender seems to want. One such response is, "Part of you seems to be feeling like a very critical and disapproving parent to yourself," or "I hear a lot of self-disapproval (or self-disgust) in what you are saying." There are many ways of expressing this perception that the Sender does not get much approval or affirmation or nurturance from himself or herself, and so lives constantly in a self-perpetuated environment that erodes his or her self-esteem and self-confidence.

Repeated messages. Sometimes the repetition of a message gives signficiance to a statement that might otherwise be unremarkable. If I hear from my wife, "You remind me of my father," I might not attach any particular significance to the statement. If, however, during the same discussion-particularly if it is a heated discussion—I hear the same statement once or twice more, I might begin to hear not only that I remind my wife of her father, but also that she has certain feelings towards me because of this reminding, and perhaps even that she is having difficulty in distinguishing her perception of me from her perception of her father.

Selective feedback generally. The foregoing discussion by no means exhausts the varieties of hidden but significant messages that a skilled active listener can pick up and reflect back to give the Sender a view of the significance of his or her messages that he and she may never have had before. The result may be, and often is, a constructive and sometimes dramatic shift in the direction of the Sender's narrative and self-perception.

PART THREE

No-Lose Problem Solving

7

Preliminary Steps in Resolving Conflicts

IN PART TWO, when I came to you with a problem, the problem was mine, you were not part of the problem, and in giving me the gift of active listening,you verbally or nonverbally indicated your trust that I could handle my problem. Example:

Mendel: I'm at the end of my rope with those kids.

You: Your're saying you feel utterly at a loss to know how to get them off your back.

Mendel: That's right. It's as though they and I were not even speaking the same language.

You: You try everything you know about communicating, but you feel powerless to get through to them.

Mendel: Yes, I didn't know it would be like this taking care of these children.

You: You weren't prepared for this kind of disappointment and defeat.

Mendel: I guess my expectations weren't very realistic.

You: So maybe the problem isn't only the kids' misbehavior; you're thinking it may be partly your own unrealistic expectations.

Mendel: Not just partly. The problem is *mostly* with my expectations. Those kids behave pretty normally.

In that example, you recognized that the problem was mine, and you trusted me to find my way into it and out of it.

What happens, however, if the problem is not "out there," but is in here between you and me? That is, what happens if your behavior is a problem to me? Then we may be in a conflict. There may be strong negative feelings between us. In that situation, it may not be easy or even possible for you to give me the unconditional, positive, empathic regard discussed in Part Two and implicit in the foregoing example. What do we do then?

That is what I want to look at in Parts Three and Four. To begin with, I would like to look at some preliminary steps that seem to me to be important for the success of a no-lose encounter. Experienced "fighters" may carry out these preliminary steps in a fraction of a second and may not even be aware of doing so. Those not so experienced often gain much from going consciously through the checklist that constitutes the rest of this chapter.

Who Owns the Problem?

The first preliminary step in resolving a conflict in which your behavior is a problem to me is to ask myself, "Whose problem is it?" If you carelessly spill coffee down my back, your behavior is a problem to me. Clearly, I own the problem. But if you spill coffee down my spouse's back, that in itself is not my problem; that is my spouse's problem. I am concerned for her, but the problem is hers.

In some families or other systems, this distinction is not clear. For example, a mother may say to her child, "Because you woke me up from my nap, I am going to tell your father when he comes home, and he will punish you." The unspoken rule in such situations is that the aggrieved person does not confront directly the person whose behavior is the problem. The problem is turned over to another family member who is the agreed policeperson for this purpose. Members of such families do not enjoy the satisfactions that come from direct confrontation and caring solutions. The issue becomes one of wrongdoing and punishment, not experience in empathy, intuition, and caring.

Nine-year-old Harry complains to Mother that eleven-year-old Billy keeps changing the TV channels. Or one teacher goes to the principal to complain about the behavior of another teacher, or one employee goes to the boss to complain about another employee. For simplicity, let's stick to Harry's complaint against Bill. Mother goes in and commands Billy to stop changing the channels. Billy responds defensively and argumentatively, and Mother imposes a solution. In that environment, Harry and Billy do not learn to resolve their problems so that both can win. They learn that disputes are resolved by higher authority—arbitration, lawsuit, or warfare—or by deceit, treachery, threat, or power. In any of those approaches, somebody loses. And whenever one partner in a relationship loses, both partners lose (see chapter 1).

Letting Children Own Their Problems

If Billy's behavior in changing TV channels is a problem to Harry, it is Harry who owns the problem. Harry has an opportunity to learn valuable lessons connected with his problem. One is that he can choose among three approaches to problem solving. He can count himself in and count the other person out (the authoritarian approach). He can count himself out and count the other person in (the permissive or martyr approach). Or he can count both himself and the other person in (the consensual approach).

If he counts himself in and counts Billy out (blames, accuses, threatens, commands), Billy may feel as though he is going to be a loser, and will probably react with defensiveness and retaliation, or with hostile or resentful submissiveness. Both Harry and Billy then wind up as losers in the relatioship. If, instead, Harry counts himself out and counts Billy in, Harry will carry the hostility and resentment and the feeling of being a loser, and will soon find ways to retaliate and make Billy a loser as well. Finally, if Harry counts both himself and Billy in, asserting his own wants and needs but making sure that Billy feels heard and cared about too, both can come out feeling like winners and enriched in their relationship.

So Mother could open to Harry a rich vein of learning and skill if, before intervening, she asked herself and Harry, "Who owns the problem?" If Harry owns the problem, he has a responsibility and an opportunity too vital to be wasted. And it's logical that Harry solve his own problem. He has most of the data about the issue and the relationship (including the most relevant data of all: what they mean to him, what importance they have for him, and what feelings he has about them). He is the one who will have to implement the solution and live with it. It's an opportunity for him to build his self-confidence and sense of competence. And it's another step out of dependence and into maturity (whatever that is).

At this point in a family-counseling session, I would expect to hear Father or Mother argue, "But if I don't intervene, I'm afraid they will kill each other." Among some parents, I'm sure this fear is genuine. And undoubtedly there have been incidents in some families in which real hurt has been inflicted by brothers or sisters on one another. In my experience, however, real danger of violence in a family usually arises only because one or both parent figures have given permission for that form of behavior. Sometimes the "permission" takes the form of modeling the violence (i.e., one or both parent figures inflict hurt or violence on the other or on the children). It may take the form of nostalgic recollections of how "I was beaten when I was a kid." It may be in the form of a direct injunction ("Hit him back"). At times, the parents' fear that the children will inflict violence on one another may be perceived by the children as an expectation and thus as a kind of permission or direction.

A contrary rule or expectation is ordinarily not difficult to establish if the rule is clearly enunciated in family meetings (see Chapter 10) and reinforced by parental example.

Constructive Parental Interventions

Does this mean that parents are never to intervene when the behavior of one child is a problem to another? No, some interventions can be constructive. These interventions are not to impose a solution, but to facilitate the problem-solving process by the parties to the dispute. These interventions are discussed in Chapter 10. For the most part, they consist of clarifying communication, using active listening, translating into I-messages, offering perceptions (but not judgments or opinions or values), bringing out feelings, and helping to define issues and develop options for solutions.

This kind of clarifying intervention can be helpful when, for instance, a conflict arises between a child and the child's teacher or principal, or between a child and a merchant. The child owns the problem; the parent does not own the problem. For the parent to confront the teacher or principal on behalf of the child is to deprive the child of the learning experience and skill to be gained from representing herself or himself. The child may even perceive the parent's interference as a message that the child is unable to be responsible for herself or himself, or is expected to lose in the encounter.

At this point in our classes on resolving family conflicts, Marion and I have learned to expect some parents to object that some children do not have the skill or courage or "psychological size" they would need to represent themselves adequately against the superior skill and authority of the teacher or principal or merchant. Those obstacles are often real and sometimes seem overwhelming to a child. Some parents, however, have learned two other ways of intervening that leave to the child the gratification—and often the exhilaration—of working out and successfully resolving the problem.

Consultant. The parent may choose to serve as a consultant to the child. If so, his or her first function is to give the child the benefit of active listening, so that the child is encouraged to define the problem, to vent all the feelings that go along with it, to express the emotions that accompany these feelings, to explore and examine the child's readiness to confront the issue, and to take inventory of the tools available for achieving the desired outcome.

The second function of the consultant is to offer perceptions—not opinions or advice, but perceptions, experience, intuition—about the situation, the antagonists, the issues, the required skills, any need for additional information, and any nonverbal messages the consultant may be getting from the child indicating thoughts, feelings, or motivations not yet adequately explored. The child, however, must be the judge of adequacy.

The third function of the consultant is to explore with the child what the options are and which one appears to the child to be most relevant and fruitful.

Equalizer. If the child is a party to a conflict with somebody else (e.g., a sibling, a teacher, a principal, a merchant), a parent may also or instead choose to be present at the encounter between the child and the other person, in order to equalize the difference in psychological size between the antagonists. In that situation, the parent's function is similar to that described above and in Chapter 10 for facilitating hassles between siblings.

With either approach, the important learning for the child is: I own this problem; I can draw on my parents as resources in preparing for and engaging in the encounter; my parents evidently have confidence that I can resolve my own conflicts; and so, despite all my apprehensions and anxieties, I have an underlying confidence in my ability too.

Sometimes, even with the parent's assistance as a consultant, a child refuses to confront a person whose behavior is a problem to him or her. The fear may be too great, or the self-confidence too low. I do not ordinarily find it productive or desirable to push such a child into a confrontation, even by logical persuasion. Too often, the pressure on the child to overcome his or her reluctance sets up an intolerable conflict, a double bind. Seeing no way to win, whatever course he or she takes, the child may close off all feelings, resort to distracting behavior, take refuge in a private reality quite different from the reality that others perceive, or go reluctantly into the encounter, prepared to lose. In my experience, however, it is not helpful to the child in the long run to do the confronting for the child. What does seem to me to be productive— sometimes dramatically so—is to validate the child by truly empathic active listening, making sure that all feelings of fear, anxiety, incompetence, and inadequacy are freely expressed in an environment of absolute safety, and then to facilitate the child's recognition and acceptance of the fact that the decision not to confront is itself an affirmative choice of a way to handle the problem. The child has used his or her judgment and power, and is respected for it.

Many parents find it difficult to okay the child's choice to respect the fear and to avoid the confrontation. They label that choice a cop-out. If you are putting a negative value on the choice not to confront, try reversing roles. Assume that you are the one facing the prospect of confronting a person or committee that has much more power than you have, including the power of punishment and penalties. To add to your anxiety, imagine that you have had little or no experience in direct confrontation, whereas your opponents are experienced and at ease. Moreover, your language skills are greatly inferior to theirs, and, since you are a little person, most of your experience in life has been that of underdog. Given those assumptions, you yourself might or might not choose to avoid the confrontation, but you can surely see that avoidance is a legitimate option.

In summary, the first question I need to ask myself in approaching an interpersonal conflict is, "Whose problem is it?" If I own the problem, I have a right and an opportunity—and I deserve—to bring it to a resolution. If it is not my problem, the person who owns the problem has the responsibility and the right to bring it to a resolution. For persons who are handicapped in the encounter by inferior skills, lack of self-confidence, or smaller psychological size, parental intervention can be constructive if it is aimed not at rescuing the disadvantaged person or doing it for him or her, but at equalizing the disadvantage, in order to enable the person to experience his or her achievement, competence, and creativity in bringing the conflict to a resolution if one is possible. The choice of whether and how to approach a conflict belongs by right to the person affected by the problem behavior. Authoritarian and permissive methods *are* legitimate choices, even though they work poorly and undermine the relationship. Consensual approaches work better.

What is the Problem?

The second of my preliminary steps before actually initiating resolution of a conflict over behavior that is unacceptable to me is to ask myself, "What precisely is the problem?"

When my daughter was quite young, a little friend of hers had great difficulty going to sleep at night. She had to get out of bed to go to the bathroom; she needed a glass of water; she was worried about school. Parental persuasions and penalties were of no avail. The problem to them was their daughter's refusal to obey the rules about going to bed at night. To their little daughter, the problem, as it finally emerged, was the certainty that God was hiding in the wall next to her bed and was reading her secret thoughts. Faced with punishments and persuasions, she had not deemed it safe to reveal the real problem as she saw it.

To many parents, their children's lying is a problem. Their children will more likely perceive the problem to be the parents' inability to make it safe to tell the truth.

A wife may feel that her husband is not communicative enough. But the husband may feel that his wife tries too hard to invade the privacy of his mind.

The number and variety of these situations is endless: sexual frequency, the neatness of children's rooms, etc., etc. Each antagonist would define the problem in a different way.

So what are you to do if you see my behavior as a problem to you? Must you remain silent until you can see clearly that the problem as you define it is in fact the real problem?

I think it more productive of openness and intimacy in a relationship to blurt out the problem as you see and feel it, and to do so at the very moment when you see and feel it to be a problem. If you send a clear I-message and then give your partner the benefit of good active listening, as discussed in Chapter 9, the real issue will probably emerge.

Whose Behavior is the Problem?

The third of my preliminary steps before actually confronting a person whose behavior I perceive to be a problem is to ask myself, "Whose behavior is the problem?"

I could yell at my wife, "Can't you keep those darn kids quiet?" But ordinarily it is not her failure to keep those "darn kids" quiet that is the problem. The problem is the noise the kids are making. If I value straight communication, I will make my wants known not to my wife but to the kids when it's their behavior that is the real problem to me.

It may also be that the real problem is not the noise the kids are making; it may be that some other irritant is gnawing at me, and I find the kids a ready target for feelings not really related to them. At the moment of confrontation, I'm not likely to be aware of the displacement of my feelings. If, however, I follow the procedures of six-step problem solving (see Chapter 9) and do the listening called for in those procedures, it will probably become clear very shortly that the kids' behavior is not problem behavior. If I have not used blame, I can back down from my original demand. Or I might shift my ground to this: "Kids, I am very irritable tonight, and it's not about you. Because of that, your noise is a problem to me. I would like to ask you please to keep your noise at a very low level for me." The beauty in that request is that it gives the kids an opportunity to do something for the requester because they care about him or her.

How Important is the Issue to Me?

The fourth of my preliminary steps, before entering into actual problem solving, is to ask myself, "How important is the issue to me?" This is related to the fifth question, "How important is the relationship to me?"

If I like my eggs to be less well-done than my spouse usually does them for me, do I request what I want or not? If a family member squeezes the toothpaste tube from the middle and I like it squeezed from the end, do I make a request for a behavior change or not?

I have heard many family members say, "Oh, it's not important," or "It's too trivial to mention." But it turns out that these "unimportant" and "trivial" irritants, if unexpressed and unresolved, pile up as accumulated grievances, and eventually get dumped out in a big out-pouring of resentment and hostility totally out of proportion to the immediate provocation.

It has been my experience in working with dysfunctional families that some or all of the family members withhold information about their feelings, hoard grievances and resentments without bringing them to light, and discourage the expression of resentment, anger, hostility, disappointment, or frustration in other family members. As these families learn to express their feelings when they occur, no matter how seemingly trivial, they grow more functional, more intimate, more self-confident, more outgoing. They confront more issues than they did before; they allow less time to elapse between the provocation and the expression of their feelings; and they raise more of the issues that they regard as "minor." Many of these families find, to their surprise, that the fights over these minor issues turn out to be minor fights—not really fights at all—contrasted with the "bad old days" in which every fight was major because it contained such a lot of "gunny-sacked" garbage. I see over and over again that the most functional, nurturing, and rewarding relationships are those in which the partners are the most open, real, congruent, and spontaneous in expressing their thoughts, feelings, emotions, moods, fantasies, and motivations.

So my rule of thumb has become, as the importance of the relationship increases, so does the importance of confronting relatively minor issues (see Figure 7.1). I have heard it asserted that, as love grows, the

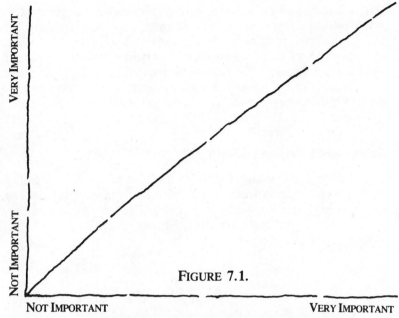

FIGURE 7.1.

NOT IMPORTANT   VERY IMPORTANT
Relative importance of confronting "trivial" issues

tolerance and acceptance of the partners' actions ought to grow. I can
say only that it doesn't work that way. The more intimate the relationship, the greater the number and frequency of "minor" issues that can
become irritants. So if the question is, "How important is this issue to
me?" the answer is to ask, "How important is the relationship?"

How Important is the Relationship to Me?

The fifth question I want to ask myself before actually beginning a
problem-solving encounter with someone is, "How important is this
relationship to me?" This is related to the fourth question, "How
important is this issue to me?"

The question of how important the relationship is can be forgotten in
the heat of a battle over the content of a conflict. It is sometimes easy to
forget that whether you take off your shoes at a formal party may be
important to me precisely because I care about you and about what you
do. Isn't it strange, then, that in fighting over what you do, we might
damage the very relationship that makes what you do important to me?

In some families I hear one or more members say that the relationship
is so important that they don't want to risk conflict by asking for
changes in objectionable behavior. My prognosis for those relation-

ships is that they will become increasingly dysfunctional as gunny sacks full of withheld resentments and grievances grow more and more full and approach the bursting point. As symbolized in Figure 7.1, the more important the relationship, the more important it becomes to be open and spontaneous about so-called minor grievances.

In addition to raising these issues, however, it is necessary to bring them to resolutions in which both parties feel like winners, as discussed in Chapter 9.

Can I Fight Fairly and Effectively?

The sixth and last step I want to take before opening a conflict-resolving encounter is to ask myself, "Can I fight fairly?" If I can, I am ready to begin the encounter. If not, I had better wait, unless I am willing to damage the relationship by fighting unfairly.

8

Fair Fighting

FIGHTING doesn't have to be dirty. It doesn't even have to be "fighting" in the sense of hurting and doing injury. Fair fighting between intimates and associates is "for better understanding, not for knockouts," as George Bach and Peter Wyden say in *The Intimate Enemy: How to Fight Fair in Love and Marriage*. Neither partner can win unless both win (as discussed in Chapter 1).

By living with Marion, I give her the power to hurt me. The trusting, confidential nature of our relationship gives her such knowledge and information about my doubts, weaknesses, actions, and history that she knows precisely where the hurting points are and how to hit them. And she entrusts me with reciprocal knowledge and power.

I give Marion another kind of power also. I look to her for validation, for messages that I am basically okay, for the reinforcement of my self-esteem. If I do not get that from her, my self-esteem suffers, and my place in the world is likely to feel painful, shaky, and possibly intolerable.

To guard against these hurts, we can cut down on our trust and openness with each other. But if we aren't open with each other, if we don't trust enough to expose our vulnerable points, we don't have an intimate relationship (no matter how good our sex life is). We have, instead, a guarded, cautious, limited living arrangement with a stranger whom we see as a potential threat. I will not settle for that. I want to give and get as much trust, disclosure, peace, confidence, and security as is possible between two human beings.

I believe such blessings are possible for me if I work with my partner to get them. And I work most effectively with my partner when I put myself fully into the encounter—including my anger, my fear, my jealousy, my distrust, whatever is real for me at that moment—and when I use tactics that are healing and bonding rather than wounding or alienating.

Here are some of the rules for effective fighting that I have found useful for myself and for families and couples with whom I have worked.

Effective Fight Principles

Commitment and Genuineness

For me, the top of the list for turning conflicts and disagreements into healing, bonding, enriching encounters is for each of the partners to be fully, congruently, and authentically involved in and committed to the process of defining the problem and resolving it constructively because they value the relationship and each other.

What is ineffective and unfair is to withhold real feelings, to be passive about bringing the issue to clarity and resolution, to be unconcerned with the partner's feelings, to leave the issue unresolved, to have no clear commitment to bring it to a later resolution, to display an attitude of disengagement, or to use evasive tactics. It is also unfair to discount or deny the partner's real feelings or the importance of those feelings to the partner.

What is fair is to be authentic about feelings and congruent about expressing them, to be active in bringing the issue to clarity and resolution, to show concern for the partner's feelings and for the importance of the relationship, and to contribute to a climate in which the partner can feel relatively safe in being open and real.

Responsibility

One night, I returned home from Los Angeles much later than Marion had expected me. When I walked in the door, she was calling the sheriff and was in tears. She might have blamed me for causing her worry. She might have insisted that her recollection of our arrangement was right and mine was wrong. She might have withheld any clear expression of her anger and resentment but punished me in indirect ways like hostile silence. But she did not do any of these things. Instead, she tearfully owned her fear and worry plus the love on which they rested. She expressed her understanding of the arrangement on which she had based her expectation that I would arrive earlier. She took responsibility for having possibly misunderstood my communications about arrival time. She expressed her anger clearly without indicating that I caused it. And she expressed a firm desire for us to agree on a plan that would make repetitions of that incident less likely to occur.

What is unfair is blaming, asserting that the partner is responsible for my feelings, making the partner "wrong" and me "right," leaving it to the partner to discern my feelings or to initiate a resolution, and putting the onus "out there," by saying, "You shouldn't" instead of "I want," or "The kids were upset," instead of "I was upset."

What is fair is owning my feelings, thoughts, values, and perceptions as my own, and taking full responsibility for bringing the issue to clarity and resolution.

Being Ready to Change

There is a fine line between stubbornly, rigidly refusing to make any concessions and, on the other hand, standing firmly for what you are and what your limits are.

What is unfair is putting all responsibility for change on the other, resisting any kind of change, insisting that the status quo is acceptable, or taking a take-it-or-leave-it stance.

What is fair is joining in seeking ways to bring about a sense of winning on both sides, showing an open-minded willingness to bring about change in the relationship or in oneself, making it safe for the other to change without fear of I-told-you-so, making a definite decision to change, coupled with a commitment to implement the decision, and recognizing and encouraging desired changes when they do take place.

What is unwise and usually unworkable is to undertake to have different feelings or not to show real feelings. What is difficult but not impossible is a shift in values.

Making Equal Space for the Partner

If each partner is to emerge from the fight feeling like a winner, each will see the value in making sure that the other does not feel at a disadvantage in making her or his wants, feelings, attitudes, thoughts, values, and perceptions known, and in having them fully heard and considered. In an encounter between a parent and a child, the parent has a lot more psychological size or weight than the child has. If no compensation is made for this difference, the child may feel overwhelmed and may present less than his or her full wants and feelings. The outcome then is likely to be less than satisfactory to the child, and consequent resentments may be expected to undermine the solution apparently reached and possibly to raise other issues for resolution.

Other examples of differences in size, weight, skill, and power are: in verbal skill; in loudness of voice; in economic power, such as in the power to fire the partner; in physical size; in the present level of fatigue or health.

What is unfair is allowing the inequality to go uncorrected. What is super-unfair is to exploit the difference at the expense of the disadvantaged partner.

What is fair is equalizing the respective positions, sizes, and strengths of the partners. Some teachers and parents sit or stoop or kneel when confronting a child, in order to equalize the difference in eye level.

Respect

This element relates to the First Principle stated in Chapter 1, the principle of making it possible for each party to the conflict to be "right." You score highly under this heading when you recognize and support the other person's individuality, "rightness," and "okayness." You score low when you belittle, denigrate, or discount the other person, or make that person "wrong." I am very impressed by fair fighters who take a step back from the issue itself now and then, in order to look at whether the tactics being used are healing or alienating, and who make a genuine effort to get the fight back on a constructive track without in the slightest attributing to the other person the responsibility for any negative elements that may be getting in the way.

Keeping the Issue Real

What is it that we are fighting about? Is it a real issue, or is it manufactured, contrived, manipulative, or insincere? Some antagonists have been known to pick a fight for a hidden or ulterior purpose, such as avoiding sex or inducing guilt in order to gain the upper hand in some other dispute. Some fighters, fearing to confront, displace the anger onto the kids.

What is unfair is making false accusations, faking injury or feelings, denying the other's reality, bringing trumped-up charges, harboring ulterior motives, or using the charges to make the partner wrong.

What is fair is disclosing one's real feelings, values, and issues, and confronting the person or persons whose behavior is the problem.

Keeping the Issue Specific and Solvable

If behavior of yours that is going on right now has practical effects on me that I don't like, I can make a clear request of you to change your behavior. I can make the issue unclear if I add other behaviors from other times (notably, old resentments I have been storing in my gunny sack), or if I use my charges to back up a demand that you change your character or your feelings. I can also muddy the waters if I don't know clearly what I want or if the want I express is unclear.

Martha said she wanted more time with her husband, and objected to the quality of the times they did have together. In the course of a constructive fight with him, she discovered that what she really wanted was not more time but more focus, attention, and genuine concern. Kathy cried bitterly that her husband did not love her as much as she loved him. She wanted him to change his feelings, and realized only after many sessions that she was asking him to be a different person than he was.

What is ineffective is being unclear about the outcome desired, combining issues, bringing in past hurts and grievances, focusing on who did what rather than on feelings and the relationship, and demanding character changes or changes in values.

What is effective is keeping the issue clear, separating it from other issues, and focusing on modifiable behaviors in the here and now.

Communicating Clearly

The elements of effective communication are discussed in Part Two. Here I want to extract from that discussion the following basics of effective and ineffective fighting.

What is effective is making all parts of the message (words, tone of voice, inflection, facial expression, posture, other body expressions, silence, and context) consistent with one another and congruent with your real feelings; sending the message so that it is understandable to the Receiver; feeding back your perception of the message sent by your partner to make sure you are getting the message intended; and using your knowledge of active listening.

What is ineffective is sending inconsistent or discrepant or incongruent messages, sending messages not within the Receiver's comprehension, or assuming that the message you got was the message sent without checking it out. It is also unfair to use feedback or active listening in a sarcastic or derogatory manner, or deliberately to distort the message received.

Some Unfair Fight Tactics

Hitting Below the Belt

A belt line is an individual level of tolerance. Below that line blows are felt to be intolerable. Partners in an intimate relationship are likely to know their partners' levels of tolerance. Hitting below the belt is therefore a breach of trust.

Belt lines differ with each individual. Some partners feel devastated by screaming or yelling; others feel swear words to be beyond their capacity to absorb; still others feel overwhelmed by the hostile, punishing "silent treatment."

For a person to respect a partner's belt line, he or she needs to know where it is; so each person needs to disclose his or her belt line frankly, honestly, and openly. Stating that one's belt line is higher than it actually is, in order to be able to charge the partner with unfair fighting, is itself an unfair tactic. An example of an unfairly high belt line is that of an individual who pretends to be on the verge of a heart attack if anyone ventures the slightest disagreement. This is not to say that if your partner's belt line is higher than most, it is therefore unfairly high. Belt lines are individual matters. What is unfairly high for one may be legitimately high for another. The test is whether the aggrieved person experiences actual hurt and real diminution of trust in the opponent's fairness and concern.

Violating an Achilles' Heel

A so-called Achilles' heel is a place where a person feels particularly vulnerable. It is a place where an attack feels destructive, psychologically, socially, or economically. Where intimacy exists, Achilles' heels are exposed. An attack on a vulnerable spot exposed in developing intimacy is therefore a betrayal of trust and a blow at the very basis of the relationship.

Achilles' heels may be faked, just as belt lines can. Sometimes, particularly in the early stages of a relationship, an Achilles' heel may be faked as a way of testing whether the other person can be trusted with a real Achilles' heel.

If a partner in an intimate relationship does resort to an attack on the partner's Achilles' heel, it may mean that the attacker is feeling resentful, threatened, or defensive that he or she is lashing out desperately. It may be worthwhile to examine not only the fairness or unfairness of the fight tactic in question, but also the underlying motivation or provocation.

Overkill

Overkill is attacking an opponent with severity and injury out of proportion to the immediate situation. Overkilling may result from accumulating grievances, withholding clear expressions of feelings when the incidents occur, until they overflow or explode when triggered by an otherwise minor incident. Gestalt practitioners refer to accumulating grievances as gunny-sacking. Practitioners of Transactional Analysis call it "saving brown stamps." When you have saved up enough brown stamps, you can trade them in for a tantrum, a destructive fight, or sometimes even a divorce or murder.

Some overkilling results not from gunny-sacking against this particular partner, but from displacing onto this partner some stored-up feelings from prior times and against other persons. A husband with stored-up resentments against his mother may react unreasonably against his wife or daughter. A woman who has been taught by her parents not to trust men may react with disproportionate suspicion and hostility against her husband or son.

Mind Reading, Ascribing Motives

I know of two kinds of mind reading. One consists of my assuming, without checking it out with you, that you are experiencing a certain feeling, emotion, thought, attitude, knowledge, or perception. The second and more virulent form of mind reading consists of my attempting to persuade you that I know better than you what you are feeling, thinking, knowing, or perceiving.

If my perception of what you are feeling, thinking, knowing, or perceiving is different from yours, I do have to trust my perceptions, because they are the only keys to reality available to me. But if my perceptions are different from what you are actually feeling, thinking, knowing, or perceiving, I constitute an extremely disconcerting environment for you. Indeed, if you are a young person, I am a crazy-making environment for you under those circumstances.

It is not unfair for me to have perceptions different from yours. It *is* unfair for me to deny the reality of your perceptions for you. It is doubly unfair for me to cast doubt on your perceptions if mine are not genuinely different or if my purpose in questioning your perceptions is to hurt you or make you wrong.

The opposite is also true: it is dirty fighting on your part to refuse to acknowledge the accuracy of my perceptions if they are in fact true for you.

Another kind of mind reading is ascribing motives. For example: "You're just saying that because you're tired," or "You don't really mean that; you're just trying to hurt me," or "You're taking that point of view because you're trying to get in solid with your boss." All this is unfair.

Monologuing

The monologuer refuses to give his or her opponent enough time for feedback and response. The frustration thus engendered can turn into resentment, hostility, and even violence.

Character Analysis, Stereotyping

This unfair fight tactic is the same as the Communication Stopper called "diagnosing or psychoanalyzing" in Chapter 5. It is the tactic of my discounting what you say by analyzing your character in a way that invalidates your conclusions or your reasoning process. Examples are: "Why should I believe what you tell me? You are a pathological liar." "Any other man would be perfectly happy with me as a wife, but you're not, because you're such a mama's boy."

Similar to character analysis is the tactic of stereotyping. Examples are: "Just like a woman (man)!" "You lawyers (teenagers, liberated women, etc.) are all alike." The effect is to depersonalize the person stereotyped.

Silence, Absence, Passive-Aggressive Tactics

Passive-aggressive tactics are those in which the fighter inflicts injury without really acknowledging that the device is a fight tactic. The silence that punishes is an example of this unfair fight style. A similar device is the absence that punishes, e.g., leaving the scene of the encounter before resolution is reached (see *hit-and-run* below), failing to come home at the usual time, protracted absence without explanation. "Forgetting" may be, and often is, a passive-aggressive device. Other behaviors sometimes used to score unfair fight points without taking responsibility for them are: being "too tired"; having a "headache"; feigning illness; taking refuge in chores or the "press of business."

Hit-and-Run

Hit-and-run tactics have been described as "getting in the last word first." The hit-and-run fighter typically makes his or her point, then slams the door before the partner can respond. In phone conversations, hanging up is substituted for slamming the door.

Indirect Attack

Eric Berne, in *Games People Play*, describes a game called "Sweetheart" in which one spouse entertains a social group by narrating an incident embarrasing to his or her partner, then winds up with, "Isn't that right, sweetheart?" The partner who is the victim of this game has a number of options, all unpleasant, including swallowing the hurt and wearing a phony smile, encountering the offending spouse in anger "in front of all those people," or withdrawing from the scene. Another kind of indirect attack is for one parent to undercut the other parent's authority with their children. A more subtle kind of indirect attck is one that seems to be supportive on its face but is undermining in its effect. An example is: "Your speech was very good, dear; I'm sure it's no fault of yours that most of the audience were not paying attention."

Games

Eric Berne describes many other "Games People Play" that are unfair fight tactics. One of these is "Corner," in which, for example, Daughter says, "Mommy, do you love me?" and Mother says, "What is love?" The answer constitutes a rejection, but at a level the child is not equipped to cope with. She is cornered.

In the game of "Uproar," fathers and their teenage daughters, for example, handle their unconscious sexual attraction for each other by engaging in angry exchanges of impudence and insult culminating in the slamming of doors.

The number and variety of games appears to be endless. Their purposes and effects are to avoid intimacy.

Physical Abuse

I classify physical abuse as an unfair tactic whether it is used by spouse against spouse, parent against child, child against parent, sibling against sibling, or just about anybody against anybody. I want to confess that I am among those who have "spanked" their children. I say this without apology, but certainly without pride or justification. To me spanking is a euphemism, a word used to whitewash some forms of physical abuse that parents use against their children. It may fall far short of what is called a "beating," and it may in no way approach the sick violence suffered by children who are the victims of intentionally inflicted burns, fractures, and the like. Nevertheless, I believe spanking to be physical abuse and an unfair fight tactic, injurious to the relationship and to the self-esteem of both participants. Why then have I used it? Because I was feeling frustrated and ineffective, had run out of options that I knew to try, and was very much in my internal Child, with a boost from that part of my internal Parent that experienced parental spankings during my growing-up years. I offer that explanation only as it may contribute to making sense out of what I did, not as a justification. (For further discussion of punishment and discipline, see Chapter 12.)

Sex as a Weapon

I see sex unfairly used as a fight tactic in two ways. One way is to withhold sex as a punishment. The other is to use it hostilely and contemptuously as a way of humiliating the partner. When I see the place of sex in functional families, I see it used as one of a host of communications and experiences in which the partners share and join, to their mutual and reciprocal delight and satisfaction. If at any time sex is transformed into a weapon, it may long thereafter be perceived as a possible future threat; and something then goes out of the experience that is extremely difficult to recapture.

I am not asserting that saying *No* to a sexual invitation is unfair. If I am experiencing sexual desire and you are not, your *No* is legitimate and important. Only if your intention is punishing is your *No* unfair.

Humor

Levity can bring relief and add perspective if both participants can join in it. On the other hand, it may be sent or received as a way of avoiding the issue or of putting the other person down. Sometimes the jocularity is unintended, as happened during a bitter fight between my first wife and me. In a voice trembling with anger, she said to me, "You've had opple amportunity . . . !" (meaning, of course, ample opportunity), and we both cracked up with laughter, to our great relief.

Fair Fight Rules

You have become aware of discomfort. You have traced your discomfort to one or more of my behaviors. You have clarified within yourself that: (a) you own the problem; (b) my behavior is the problem; (c) the issue and the relationship are both important to you; and (d) you can fight fairly. Now you are ready to confront me in order to get what you want in a way that will strengthen the relationship.

The six-step problem-solving sequence is discussed in Chapter 9. But these steps are facilitated by observing some fair fight rules, as follows.

Obtain Partner's Agreement to Encounter

"Marion, I'm experiencing some discomfort over a behavior of yours, and I would like to work it out with you. Are you in a place to do that now?"

This is one of a limitless number of ways to open a problem-solving encounter. There are no right or wrong words. The essence of the opening words is that they invite an agreement to engage in problem solving. The implied message in seeking agreement is that, even though

I am hurting, I care enough about you to respect your readiness or lack of readiness. I also render myself more effective in getting what I want; if I begin before my partner is ready, I create a needless obstacle for myself. My partner may have an urgent need to go to the bathroom, or may have a sick headache, or may have something burning on the stove, or may be deeply preoccupied with another problem, or may be urgently hungry, or may be too angry with me to fight fairly just now. These distractions create an environment not at all favorable to my purposes. It is better for me to learn about them before I begin my fight.

Agree on Time

If Marion says yes, she is in a place to hear my message now, no problem. If she says no, I find it useful to try to get an agreement on when we can have our encounter. Then I don't feel as though I have been simply put off. When it is Marion or the kids or somebody else who is having a problem with my behavior, and I am not ready for a fight right then, I like to propose a time rather than wait for them to try to pin me down. When I do that, they seem to get the message that I care about them enough to want not to avoid working out the problem.

Agree on Ground Rules

The conditions that disputants may consider important vary from person to person, couple to couple, group to group, issue to issue, and even from time to time with the same people or issue. For example, for some couples, or at least for one individual in some couples, it may seem important to have the fight out of earshot of the children. Some find it desirable to have friends present; others not. I have known loving couples who preferred to have their fights in bed, whereas others, equally loving, preferred not to "contaminate the sheets." Members of some families have found it inadvisable to try to resolve conflicts when one or more members of the family have been drinking. Others find liquor to be a leveler or relaxant. Individuals differ widely on where they prefer to fight: some wives prefer the kitchen, where they feel more in charge; some partners prefer their offices, for similar reasons; some teenagers prefer their newly acquired cars.

Some partners need rules against yelling. Some find it difficult to endure swearing. Some need agreements to turn off the television, put down the knitting, give full focus.

Recesses or intermissions may be needed, whether for rest from exhaustion, for surcease from pain, for the demands of work the next day, or for whatever reason seems important.

Not all these needs can be anticipated at the opening of the fight. What can be anticipated is that unanticipated needs may make intermissions necessary, and the partners can agree in advance that it is fair to interrupt the fight at any time to consider the rules of the fight.

The Right to Say No or Yes, to Counteroffer, to Get More Information

The right—indeed, the necessity—to say "I want" (see Chapter 2) implies the right and necessity to say "I don't want." Essential in every relationship is a clear understanding that the receiver of an I-want message has the unquestioned right to respond in (at least) four ways: (1) yes, (2) no, (3) counterproposal, or (4) request for more time or information.

To say "I want" is to give information useful to the relationship. To fail to express an existing want is to withhold information useful to the relationship. So the rules of the system need to encourage the expression of a want. To encourage the expression of a want requires the existence of a rule that "I want" can be freely expressed without incurring disapproval for expressing the want, and without binding the receiver to grant the wish.

The reciprocal rule is that "No" can be expressed without incurring disapproval. To be sure, the requester may experience disappointment, rejection, hurt, or resentment on hearing "No." To minimize this result, the requester, in saying "I want," would do well to make clear the importance of the behavior being requested and the feelings accompanying the request. The receiver's response is not fully informed without these items of information. Even with this information, however, the response may still be "No." And the requester may feel hurt. The requester's hurt is not the responsibility of the responder. The responder's responsibility is to respond congruently, honestly. At the same time, the responder can show concern for the requester's hurt by putting his or her "No" into a gentle form and by accompanying it with expressions of concern.

With a genuine request, the requester counts himself or herself in. With a genuine response, the responder counts herself or himself in. With these genuine inputs, the parties have the information they need to work out a consensus in which each feels counted in.

Take an example:

Jean: On the mornings when we have breakfast together, I would like you to put your newspaper aside.

Gale: I'd like to have more information about what this means to you.

Jean: I treasure our times together. They seem all too few, and the demands on our attention seem too many. I miss you, and I want more of you. When you prefer your paper over me, I feel hurt and rejected.

Gale: I hear your love message and I treasure it, but I would like to show my love—and get it—in other ways, at other times. I want to say no to you for now, and work out a way for both of us to feel counted in.

Jean (cries): That really hurts. I know you have a right to say no, but my little internal Child feels lonely now.

Gale: When I see your tears, I feel guilty. I want to do something for your hurt Child.

Jean: Just saying that helps. But please don't act out of guilt. If you are not true to what you want, we may have to live with your frustration and resentment.

Gale: I know that, so let's find a way that we can both get what we want . . .

From such a point as this, Jean and Gale can go on to find solutions in which each can feel like a winner. (For an example, see Chapter 13.)

9

Six-Step Problem Solving

HAVING TAKEN the preliminary steps discussed in Chapter 7, and having satisfied yourself that you can fight fairly as discussed in Chapter 8, you are ready for the six-step problem-solving method of resolving family conflicts. The assumption underlying the six-step method is that, when my behavior is a problem to you, there are two things that you want. One is to resolve the conflict in terms of its content. The other is to strengthen the relationship, which happens when both participants emerge feeling like winners. We both feel valued, and we experience no resentment or disgruntlement over the outcome.

Box 9.1 gives the basic road map for six-step, no-lose, problem solving.

Box 9.1. Six-Step Problem Solving.

(1) Define the Problem:

    (A) I-message

        (1) When I see (hear, etc.) . . .

        (2) The practical effects on me are . . .

        (3) I feel . . .

        (4) I want . . .

(When I-message is sent to you)	*(When you send I-message)*
(B) Active Listen.	(B) Expect defensive response;
	(C) Active Listen.

(2) Brainstorm possible solutions.

(3) Evaluate proposed solutions generated by brainstorming.

(4) Choose solution by consensus.

(5) Put the chosen solution into effect.

(6) Review and reevaluate.

Let's look more closely at each of the points in it to see how to use them with maximum effectiveness and satisfaction to yourself, the other, and the relationship.

(1) Define the Problem

The problem is defined by use of an I-message plus the process of active listening. What is implied in the use of this method is the realization that "I am entitled to count myself in on this relationship (by use of the I-message). It is also important to me to count you in (by use of active listening)."

The problem is defined not only in terms of the offensive behavior, but also in terms of the feelings of the disputants. If feelings are not considered, you will more probably get stuck arguing about content. When feelings are included in the definition of the problem, each party has reason to consider not only the merits and demerits of the questionable behavior, but also the importance of the relationship and of the other person, and the opportunity to care about the other person.

(A) I-message

An I-message is different from a you-message. "You are a liar" is a you-message. "I don't believe you" is an I-message. Another you-message is, "You're not listening to me." That statement translated into an I-message becomes, "I don't feel heard." In an I-message the sender "owns" the problem, the perception, and the feeling. In a you-message the sender puts the power "out there," in the form of blame. Blame is likely to increase defensiveness on the other side. When you want a change in the other's behavior, it makes good sense to send the message in a form that will result in as little defensiveness and resistance as possible.

Broken into its components, the I-message has four parts: (1) a description of the problem behavior, "owning" the perception and forgoing blame; (2) a brief description of the practical effects; (3) a statement of the feelings aroused by the offensive behavior; and (4) a clear statement of what change in behavior is wanted, but not in the form of a resistance-arousing demand. Here is an example of an I-message.

"Joe, when I see you track mud onto the kitchen floor and I know I'm going to have to clean it up, even though you try your best to clean it, I feel uncared for, and I get a tired feeling in my stomach. I want a promise from you that you will either get all the mud off your shoes before you come into the house or that you will take your shoes off before coming in."

Contrast this with a you-statement: "Joe, you just tracked up my floor with mud. You don't care about me at all. Clean it up right now, or you'll be grounded."

The you-message is full of Communication Stoppers (see Chapter 5). The I-message lays no blame, and is designed to avoid arousing guilty or defensive feelings. It describes the offending behavior in objective language, and gives the offender an adult description of the reasons why the behavior is objectionable. It gives a congruent statement of the Sender's feelings, thus giving the Receiver an opportunity to do something for the Sender, but without saying or implying that the Receiver was guilty of "causing" those feelings. And it says clearly what changes in behavior the Sender desires.*

In describing feelings and requesting change, the Sender risks rejection. The taking of this risk is an implied message of trust, and is thus a contribution to the relationship.

Let's look again at the second part of the I-message, where the Sender describes the practical consequences of the unacceptable behavior. Sometimes the Sender finds the Receiver's behavior to be unacceptable, but can't describe any practical consequences. In families with which I work, this problem often arises when parents seek to give I-messages to their teenagers or younger children about the young-

---

*I find great merit in the concept of I-messages, and am grateful to Dr. Thomas Gordon for including them in his book *Parent Effectiveness Training*, which is where I learned about them.

sters' disorderly maintenance of their bedrooms, closets, or drawers. These parents have lots of words for their feelings of disaste, revulsion, disgust, and the like, and they can (sometimes vividly) describe how their value standards of cleanliness, neatness, orderliness, symmetry, and tidiness are offended, but seldom do they succeed in convincing themselves—let alone their children—that any *practical* consequences flow from the unacceptable behavior. This inability to identify practical consequences is sometimes an indicator that the real problem is a conflict of values. (The resolution of such value conflicts is more fully discussed in Chapter 11.)

What can you do if your partner doesn't know anything about I-messages or sends you-messages anyway? You can:

(a) retaliate with countercharges;
(b) respond defensively;
(c) try to teach or persuade your partner to use an I-message; or,
(d) active listen.

In my experience, the active-listening response is by far the most effective in strengthening the relationship. Suppose, for example, I say to you, "That's my book, and I don't want you reading it and eating chocolates at the same time. You'll get the book all smudged." If you counterattack or respond defensively, my frustration level will rise and, with it, my anger at not feeling valued in the relationship. If, instead, you object to my use of a you-message and try to get me to use an I-message (or punish me for not using it), I am likely to feel irritated at having to suspend a want of mine while we struggle over the "right" way for me to get some relief from behavior of yours that is odious to me. I could also see your emphasis on how to express my want as a one-up manipulation on your part to avoid acknowledging my want. Mistrust can result.

Using the active-listening response, you could say to me, "I hear your concern about this book. I also hear some anger against me." By "translating" your partner's you-messages into I-messages by means of active listening, you both give yourself an opportunity to address the issue directly and take the destructiveness out of the blames and attacks. You also model more effective communication.

(B) Response to I-Message

In the ideal transaction in the ideal family, your perfect I-message would be answered with expressions of concern for you and for the practical effects and feelings that follow the problem behavior. If the behavior were mine and you had sent the I-message to me, I would listen actively until I felt certain that I had uncovered the full dimensions of the problem in terms of your feelings about me and the relationship. I would continue the active listening until it appeared to me that you felt completely known and heard and valued. Then we could go quickly into the second step of no-lose problem solving, and brainstorm possible solutions.

In all likelihood, however, I would give you a defensive response instead of the acceptant active listening that you might have preferred to get. For myself, I have learned to expect a defensive response when I send an I-message, and I'm seldom disappointed in that expectation. If I expect the ideal response, I'm choosing disappointment and chagrin. In expecting the more likely defensive response, I'm prepared to deal with it without disappointment or surprise or resentment. When my behavior is the subject of an I-message sent to me, I usually have a powerful urge to respond defensively even though I know better. One reason for this is that I really care about my partner, so much that I want her not to perceive my behavior as lacking in concern or caring. I would like her to see how my offensive behavior made sense to me at the time, even though it has had effects that she doesn't like and that I may now regret. Sometimes I also feel blamed even though she does not send any words of blame. And my reasons for feeling blamed may go back to my childhood, rather than to any blame that she also may have sent. Knowing all this about myself, I can appreciate that she also may feel defensive when I send a perfect I-message. I can appreciate also that there is pain in that defensiveness. And I'm prepared to listen actively until my partner's defensiveness and pain diminish. A defensive response means, by definition, that the responder feels a need to defend himself or herself, and that felt need is virtually synonymous with a sense of being threatened. The threat perceived may be that of losing the esteem of, or suffering rejection by, the person sending the I-message. Or it may be the sense of not being known or appreciated or understood. Whatever its origin, it is usually a reflex response. It is seldom rational and seldom effective. But even though the threat itself may not be real, the feeling of being threatened is real.

My active listening to the defensive response acknowledges the reality of the feeling, even when I don't acknowledge the reality of the threat that my partner may experience.

(C) Active Listening to Defensive Responses

The principles and methods of active listening discussed in Part Two are applicable here, whether the active listening is done by the recipient of the I-message or, more likely, by the Sender of the I-message in response to defensiveness expressed by the Receiver.

Here is an example of an I-message followed by a defensive response and active listening:

Father (to 16-year-old son): Joe, when you leave the Sunday paper strewn all over the floor, the rest of us have to wade through it or step over it or pick it up ourselves or nag you to do it, and I find myself getting more and more annoyed and feeling uncared for. I'd like you to stack it up neatly when you're through with it.

Joe: Well, I don't do any worse with it than you do, Dad.

Father (resisting the reflex tendency to make a counterdefensive retort): You see me strewing my papers around the way you do?

Joe: Yes.

Father: That annoys you?

Joe: Well, it's better than not having you around at all.

Father: You don't see me around here very much?

Joe: Well, not as much as I'd like.

Father: So leaving these papers strewn around is a way of protesting against my not being around as much as you'd like?

Joe: Well, it's not a protest, exactly.

Father: But it connects up in your mind with wanting to see more of me, is that it?

Joe: Yes.

Notice that the problem as finally defined focuses on strengthening the relationship, whereas as originally stated it dealt only with newspapers and housekeeping. Without active listening, Joe's yearning for his father might not have come to light, and something enriching to both father and son might have been lost.

When is the problem defined well enough that the parties may proceed to the second step, which is brainstorming? When both parties feel that it is defined well enough. I am not making a joke in giving this circular definition. Only the person sending the I-message can say whether he or she feels heard well enough by the other person that the problem seems adequately defined. Similarly, only the person making the defensive response can say that the underlying defensiveness has been heard well enough that it feels right to go on to the next step.

(2) Brainstorm Possible Solutions

When the problem has been adequately defined by means of an I-message and active listening, the second step in resolving a conflict so that everybody wins is brainstorming possible solutions. Brainstorming means coming up spontaneously with whatever thoughts and ideas occur, as they occur, in a kind of free-association process. Letting all ideas be brought to light, no matter how absurd they may seem at the outset, has two desirable results. One is that more satisfactory solutions may emerge. The other is that the participants feel more a part of the process and the solution.

To generate and sustain such a free flow of ideas, you will need to observe an essential ground rule: that no judgments and no values be attached to any contributions until the brainstorming stage is over and step three has begun. In a family meeting called to reconcile television times with dinner time, if the three-year-old proposed, "Buy everybody a separate television set," any deriding or dismissing of this suggestion could be experienced as devastating by its maker. Including the suggestion nonjudgmentally, on the other hand, is a message to the young contributor that he or she is a valued member of the family and of the process, and will probably encourage additional suggestions, some of which might contribute substantially to an innovative solution.

Sometimes it is useful to write down all suggestions made in the course of brainstorming. This device tends to equalize differences in "psychological size" between the parties, as when one is an adult and the other a child, or one is the boss and the other a subordinate. Equalizing differences in psychological size paves the way for full acceptance of the solution ultimately reached.

It's unsafe to assume that silence gives assent to what is going on in the brainstorming process. In family meetings or in committee meetings—and sometimes even when there are only two parties to the problem solving—it's useful to take note of nonparticipation, and it may be prudent to listen actively to the silence as a message. Silence may indicate that the silent person does not feel safe in entering into the brainstorming process. I would not, however, assume that a silent member of the brainstorming session feels unsafe without verifying this assumption. One of my ways is to say something like, "Harry, I notice that you haven't made any contribution to this brainstorming session, and I'm wondering what's in the way of your taking part." If Harry denies that anything is in the way, but I don't quite believe his denial, I will say something like, "I'm making a guess that you may not feel quite safe about just blurting whatever idea comes into your head in this environment. You may be fearing that you'll be critically judged if you don't come up with brilliant ideas. Is that true?" In making these interventions, I am trying not to put the silent member on the spot, but to uncover any problem that may be in the way of his or her participating fully. If such a problem is uncovered, we then know that our definition of the problem was not quite complete, and we need to go back to step one for further definition of the problem. When that's done, we can return to brainstorming.

When is brainstorming finished? When all participants agree that it's finished. Not until the brainstorming has come to an end by consensus can evaluation of the ideas begin.

(3) Evaluate Proposed Solutions

When the brainstorming has ended by consensus, the next step is to evaluate the contributions generated by the brainstorming process. In evaluating each contribution, it is well to remember that the problem-solving process is intended to enrich and strengthen the relationship as well as to resolve conflicts in terms of content.

Toward this end it is important to be both honest and considerate. If I value the relationship and if I value myself in the relationship, I want to be straight, direct, honest, and clear in the values and judgments I express about the ideas developed in the brainstorming session. At the same time, I don't want my judgments about an idea to be understood as negative judgments about the person who contributed that idea. Such interpretations would almost certainly generate defensive feelings that would get in the way of developing harmonious solutions. To avoid such interpretations, I would want to avoid such provocative statements as, "That's a stupid idea," or "If you cared about me, you wouldn't propose that idea."

Even when you have expressed yourself with reasonable regard for the possibility of defensive reactions, it is useful to be alert to any change of expression or other body signs that others are feeling offended or resistant in any way. One way to do this, as with checking out silent members during the brainstorming session, is to comment on the change of expression or other body signs that you have seen, ask whether it indicates any negative feelings, or express your perceptions or assumptions about what the other person is feeling and ask whether they are correct.

The purpose of the evaluation is to enable the parties to weigh pros and cons of the solutions developed in the brainstorming session, in order to narrow the choice to one that can be agreed on by all concerned. When it appears that one solution is the consensual choice of all those taking part, the evaluation is at an end.

I had an eye-opening session with the staff of an elementary school on the subject of evaluation and choosing. They had complained that their meetings were boring and unproductive; so I proposed that we have a meeting right then and see what was the matter. I no longer remember the subject matter on which they decided to hold their meeting (something about taking part in a neighborhood celebration, as I recall), but I remember that they generated a lot of energy in brain-

storming solutions. There was laughter and liveliness and broad participation. When they began evaluating, however, the energy slowly
evaporated. Soon, one turned to me and said, "See, this is how it is in
our meetings. Dull." The lack of interest was evident in their faces,
their bodies, their nonparticipation. I asked them just to feel the discomfort in their bodies for a full minute, then to say what was in the way
of their taking part energetically. At the end of the minute, one teacher
said, "I'm bored because this same subject comes up every year, and
every year we turn it down. This time, the brainstorming was fun, but I
know we're going to turn it down again, so why go through all this
evaluating?"

At hearing this, another teacher began to cry. The group fell silent.

I said, "The tears are a message. Will somebody active listen?"

Larry said, "Mary, I'm getting that you feel hurt when Dora says
we're going to turn it down again."

Mary nodded.

Dora reached over to touch Mary: "Hey, this is important to you,
isn't it?"

Again Mary nodded.

From Dora and others: "I didn't know that. You never said. That
changes everything."

Suddenly there was interest again, the evaluation proceeded with
spirit, and the meeting ended with exclamations that they had never had
such a great meeting.

What made the difference? In my perception, the vital ingredient was
the expression of feelings. It isn't enough just to list brainstormed
solutions. *The human element has to be added.* From among twelve
possible solutions, it may be boring to try to figure out which one will be
"best." But if one of those twelve is supremely important to one of the
participants, the liveliness of human relationships is added to the
choosing process. There is a chance to do something for the concerned
person.

The lesson for me is that the brainstormed list is incomplete unless it
is a "weighted" list; that is, each item needs to be labeled in some way
that indicates how important it is to the participants in the process.

(4) Choose a Solution by Consensus

Agreeing to the solution to be put into effect is the culmination of the
evaluation stage and brings that stage to an end.

What is a good way to make that choice? I suggest consensus: that is,
all participants agree positively to that solution arrived at. I see many
families, committees, and other groups using the majority vote almost

without thinking, and more often than not I see that the solution thus chosen has negative effects on the relationship. In majority vote, some members of the group are likely to see the majority as having won and the minority as having lost. The losers seem to feel that, although they are bound by the decision, they are not really committed to it by their own act. They may go along as good sports or good citizens, but their compliance carries with it an air of disgruntlement, resentment, or, at least, resignation. In business or political organizations, this can and frequently does result in overt or covert resistance.

I see greater success with consensus. By consensus I do not mean unanimity. If my group waits for unanimity on a proposal to take Shakespeare's *Merchant of Venice* off the school shelves because it offends some Jewish parents, they may wait until the end of many lives, because differences are strong and passions are high. Agreement in terms of content is probably impossible. I might, however, be willing to enter into a consensus based on my concern for both the parents who want the book removed and those who do not want it removed. Consensus can be based on the desire for an outcome in which all concerned can feel that, although they might have desired another result, they feel committed to the conclusion reached because it preserves the feeling of unity and commitment of all members to the group and to the outcome achieved.

It is sometimes objected that such a consensus is no more than a compromise, and compromises are jocularly described as solutions that leave all parties equally dissatisfied. It is precisely this dissatisfaction that true consensus avoids. The dissatisfaction produced by compromise results from the feeling on all sides that they did not get what they wanted. Compromise is a content-centered solution. The satisfaction achieved by consensus results from the feeling on all sides that in practicing give and take on the subject matter (i.e., the content), they achieved a highly desirable and satisfying result in the relationship.

Here again it is prudent to be alert for silent members, just as with brainstorming.

(5) Put the Chosen Solution into Effect

The next step in no-lose problem solving is to put the agreed solution into practice. I want to perform my part of the agreement in good faith, because I value the relationship and because I want to model the kind of performance I hope to get from the other person. Similarly, I want to make it clear in my words and actions that I expect the other person to perform in good faith.

When I say I expect the other person to perform, I'm not referring to the kind of "parental" attitude that really amounts to a strong "should" or "must" overlying an actual expectation that the other person *won't* perform unless kept under constant surveillance and pressure. I mean a confidence that the other person *will* do what we have agreed on, a confidence arising from the feeling that all parties have fully expressed their genuine feelings and have entered into an agreement which they have truly committed themselves to perform.

On the other hand, I don't consider the promises to have been written in blood. Circumstances change, and changes in circumstances frequently require changes in agreements. Promises that are considered binding even after they have become oppressive can strangle or suffocate a relationship. For this reason, the sixth step in no-lose problem solving is review and reevaluation.

(6) Review and Reevaluate

I do not accept the cynical old saw that promises are made to be broken. I believe that in well-functioning relationships, promises are made in order to be kept. To one or more parties to an agreement, changes in circumstances may make it desirable, and perhaps even necessary, to change the terms of an agreement that was perfectly satisfactory when made, and of promises that were made with a full intent that they would be carried out. Examples of such changes are that: my needs change; I change and my perception of the world changes, and in that sense you are no longer the person who entered into the agreement; the situation changes; our perception of the value of the agreement changes as we experience it in performance and practice. So with experience and with changes in circumstances, promises to which commitment was once fully given can become burdensome, and their continued performance can become accompanied by resentment, reluctance, and erosion of the relationship.

When this occurs one option is to try to hold the person to the promise. This can be accompanied by all sorts of pressures, such as appeals to reason ("If we go through the whole process again, we'll just come out with the same result") or to fairness ("But you promised, and everybody else has performed relying on your promise"), blame ("You just can't be relied on") or coercion ("If you don't do it, you'll be grounded").

What is of far more value to the relationship, and has a far greater chance of getting a mutually desirable result, is the option of subjecting the agreed-on solution to constant review and reevaluation to see whether it continues to serve the perceived interests of all members of the relationship. Under this design, whenever a member of the relationship begins to feel the previously agreed-on solution to be burdensome, expression of this feeling is to be seen as the emergence of a new problem and as an invitation to engage in six-step problem solving, beginning with step one. This is not a reopening of the old problem that had been resolved; it is in truth the emergence of a new problem. The new problem is that one (or more) of the promisors now sees the arrangement, in the light of new experience and changed circumstances, to be burdensome, and is confident in the well-functioning relationship that the other members are sympathetically interested in his plight and are concerned about his feelings toward both the task and the other members of the relationship.

Application to Some Common Situations

Let's try now to apply this six-step method to the dispute between John and Jane introduced in Chapter 4. As reported there, John came home at 8 P.M., much later than Jane had expected him, and Jane was upset. Without reviewing the example given there of how to hurt each other and damage the relationship, let's move directly to a dialog as it might be if John and Jane were aware of their process and relatively skilled at using it.

Dialog	Process
Jane (as John walks in): Oh, John, I've been so worried.	Jane begins her I-message with her feelings, which is perfectly OK as a variation on the order discussed above in this chapter.
John: I can see your concern. You've been crying, haven't you?	
Jane: Yes, I have. When I know you get off work at 5 and I don't hear from you until 8, all kinds of thoughts race across my mind; dinner gets cold; I start wondering whether to call the police or the hospitals ...	John makes a nondefensive response. Jane makes her I-message more complete, adding a description of the problem behavior and some practical effects.
John: You feel helpless to know what to do.	Active listening.

Dialog	*Process*
Jane: And now I'm getting more and more angry.	Jane adds to the feeling part of her I-message. Still active listening.
John: Too worried before to feel the anger. Now with the crisis over, you can let the anger out.	
Jane: What in the world were you doing?	Dominated by her internal Child, Jane resorts to fact-finding, which is a Communication Stopper.
John: I feel myself getting defensive when you demand explanations from me.	John makes a process comment.
Jane: I don't want to do that, but I do want to know that this matters to you.	John's process comment helps Jane get a little more into her Adult. She gets back to her I-message.
John: It matters very much to me.	
Jane: Then it's hard for me to make sense and order out of what you did.	This time Jane owns her bewilderment instead of fact-finding.
John: I'd like to tell you what happened.	
Jane: I'd like to hear what happened. And I also want some reassurance for the future.	By shifting to what happened instead of staying with what is happening (Jane's feelings), John risks getting stuck in acrimony over content instead of paying attention to the relationship.
John: What I want to say about the future is that it's important for me to anticipate any anxiety you might feel before it happens . . .	Jane completes her I-message with "I want."
Jane (softening): I really know that about you.	John stays in the here and now, which is where the relationship transaction is.
John: . . . and to let you know ahead of time if I'm going to be late. If I don't let you know, it's because I simply can't.	

Dialog	Process

Jane: I know that too. The Adult part of me says if you don't let me know, it's because you can't. That's what gets my fears going: "What's keeping John from calling?"

John: And then all your fears bubble up.

Jane: Yes. *(pause)* John.

John: Yes?

Jane: I don't need to hear what happened. We haven't been talking about that anyway. We've been talking about the caring and trust levels between us, haven't we?

John: Yes.

Jane: And we're on solid ground when it comes to caring and trust.

John: I agree.

Jane: But now, I'd like to hear whether you're all right and whether you have any feelings that you'd like me to hear.

Doubters in our classes and in the families who come to us characteristically respond in two ways on hearing a transaction like the preceding: one way is to scoff, the other is to express feelings of inadequacy. The scoffers protest that the transaction doesn't sound real; it is too unlike the abrasive fights they are used to. The others express fear that they will never master the skills necessary to keep their fights productive, growthful, and healing. In both groups, those who persevere with the learning and with their efforts eventually know the gratification and wonder of greater skill and more gratifying results.

These results can also be experienced between parents and children, even very young children. In Chapter 1 we mentioned some of the problems that accompany attempts at toilet training. I would like here to consider such episodes and conflicts and to apply our six-step method to them.

In my experience, many attempts at toilet training are disastrous to both the parent and the child. The parent is unsure about what is "right" and about what will work. The child is so traumatized that negative effects continue to appear for the rest of the victim's life.

I want to confess that I don't know what is "right." It may be, as I sometimes hear, that children "should" be trained early. It is certainly convenient for the parents. It makes the child feel proud or competent or at least more socially acceptable. Or so the argument goes. On the other hand, it may be, as I sometimes hear, that children "should" be trained only when they are ready. This is necessary for the child's sense of autonomy. Or so the argument goes. As I say, I don't know what is "right."

But I have had some experiences with how various approaches work. Because of that experience, I have come to favor the application of six-step problem solving to toilet training. And I see that method as producing benefits for the parent, the child, and the relationship.

At some point in the parent-child relationship, the parent, in effect, sends an I-message to the child, saying, in nonverbal behavior, "Your behavior is a problem to me. When you dirty your diapers, I have to clean you up so that you won't smell and your skin won't suffer. When you do this at will, without regard for my convenience, I feel uncared for, counted out. And I want you to learn to do your eliminating into the toilet and not into your diapers."

Hardly ever is the message communicated in these words or in any words at all. Many children are too young to understand word messages when the parent is ready to begin the toilet-training process. But, in essence, this kind of thought, feeling, perception, and intent are present in a caring parent-child relationship when the parent decides to institute toilet training. I am told by some parents that they actually say similar words to their infants, not on the assumption that the words themselves will have meaning to the young Receiver, but in the conviction that the infant does receive the relationship messages conveyed by the combination of words, touching, body attitudes, tone of voice, facial expression, and actions. I'm convinced that the parent's true messages are conveyed accurately to the child in these ways. If the parent is annoyed at having to clean up diapers, this message gets through to the child in some way. If the parent wants the child to change, this message gets through. If the parent is determined to effect change, this message gets through. If the parent is willing to count himself or herself in and also to count the child in, that message also gets through.

And the child responds with happy acquiescence, confident refusal, fearful compliance, or stubborn defiance, depending on how well the parent has been able to engage the child in the process of mutual or democratic decision making as distinguished from permissive or authoritarian methods. And the consequences for the self-esteem of both parties may last the lifetimes of both participants.

Let's consider the young father or mother sending a verbal or non-verbal message similar to that imagined above. If the parent is determined that the baby *shall* be toilet-trained, that determination will probably be communicated to the child. If, instead, the parent is willing for the child's wishes and readiness and feelings to be taken into account, much strain can be eliminated from the process and the relationship, and the child's self-esteem will be strengthened.

Having said the opening words to himself or herself and perhaps to the child, the parent looks for a sign that the child is going to urinate or defecate. Seeing that intention communicated by the body signs sent by the child, the parent removes the diaper and seats the child on a toilet of appropriate size. This is the action accompanying (and actually constituting) the I-message.

It would be useful for the little person to feed back his or her perception of the message to make sure that the message received was the same as the message sent. But this is not likely to occur. Instead, the child will indicate its perception of the message in other ways. Laughter may indicate that the message is perceived as, "Let's play." Tears may indicate perception of the message as, "I'm angry with you." A startled reaction may indicate an inability to make sense out of the message sent by the parent.

So the first step after sending the I-message is to observe how the child received it. If the parent is satisfied that the message has been received as it was sent, the next step is to see what the child's response is. As in any other type of conflict resolution, the Receiver of the I-message has a right to say yes or no, to make a counterproposal, or to ask for more information or more time.

If the child, in effect, says no, this answer separates the authoritarian parents from the democratic parents. The authoritarians are determined to achieve a certain result. Six-step conflict resolution is not for them. They believe that infants do not have the information needed to make an informed choice and are necessarily too narcissistic to join in seeking an outcome in which the parent as well as the child can be counted in. The democratic parents, for the most part, are more willing to give signals that this is a participative process, that they want to help the child grow in its ability to participate in mutual decision making and to be acceptantly aware of the rights and feelings of all family members. These lessons are not soon learned. What is learned, however, at a visceral level is: "The grown-ups in my life respect me. I am worthy of respect. Giving respect is the model for behavior in my family.

"I will not be coerced. I am safe here.

"I am encouraged to recognize and pay attention to the needs of my body. My parents' demands do not work at cross-purposes to my body's demands. I can make sense out of my world.

"I get good strokes when I do something for somebody. I can do it as a gift, gladly, and not under pressure, fearfully, or resentfully."

I see these "democrats" also as pragmatists. Kids can defeat their parents in some of these power struggles. Better to ride the horse in the direction it is going.

So there sits your little person on the potty, not producing as you would like. Let us call this behavior the "defensive response" which we have learned to expect after an I-message. And we have learned, when a defensive response is sent, to use active listening (verbally or nonverbally or both). The ensuing dialog might be:

Parent: I get that you don't want to do it in the potty today. Is that right?
Child: Down?
Parent: You might be ready some other day but not today.
Child: Down?
Parent: Today you want to say no to me.
Child: Down?
Parent: I'm disappointed. Changing your diapers is not pleasant for me today, but I respect your right to control your body. *(Taking the child off)* Maybe next time.

Some parents would see this situation as one in which the parent lost. They might see it as a permissive transaction, with the parent counting himself or herself out. If you are one of those parents, you might do better to follow a process in which you feel more like a winner, if you can do without getting into a power struggle from which either you or the child must come out losing. This balance point is not always easy to find. At one extreme, the child wins in terms of content and the parent loses, storing up frustration and resentment. At the other extreme, the parent wins in terms of content and the child loses, experiencing frustration, resentment, and diminished self-esteem.

Somewhere in between, at a point of balance unique to each parent-child pair, is an outcome in which one or the other can break the deadlock over content by shifting to a win-win solution in terms of the relationship. In the example given above, the parent (let us assume) sees enough value in supporting the child's autonomy to compensate for the inconvenience of changing diapers. The child rewards this shift with smiles. Another parent might try to get into the second step of our six-step method. A way of brainstorming might be:

Parent: I hear you say, "Down." I will take you down in one minute. Okay?

Child: Down.

Parent: You sound pretty firm.

Child (reaches up).

Parent: You go in the potty this time, and next time you can go in your diapers.

Child: Now.

Parent: You want down now.

Child: Now.

In this scenario, I want to leave you with frustration. Active listening and six-step problem solving are not designed to be the manipulator's ideal tool for achieving outcomes of content that she or he wants. They don't always work that way. Their value lies in what they can achieve for the relationship, by strengthening the relationship and the self-esteem of both participants when there is a deadlock over content.

Here we have a deadlock over both content and process. The participants cannot agree on whether the child shall go in the potty (content), and they cannot agree on whether to go through the six-step process for resolving the conflict (process). Yet they can make room in the relationship, at least for now, for these differences to exist.

10

Unspoken Rules and Family Meetings

EVERY HUMAN SYSTEM, no matter how large or small, has unspoken rules, even a system as small as a relationship between two persons. For example, anyone who has watched a basketball game on television or in person has undoubtedly seen the players swat one another on the rear end as a gesture of approval or encouragement. This gesture usually takes place only in the presence of a rule permitting that particular communication. If a total stranger were to come up to you and pat you on the behind, he or she would risk your hostility and perhaps retaliation. The "rules" do not permit such behavior between strangers. Even among acquaintances, the rules seldom permit such behavior across sex lines. Suppose I am acquainted with Mrs. Amplebottom only through our work together in the Parent-Teachers Association, but I greet her with a resounding whack at the next meeting of our committee. Outwardly at least, she would be incensed. Indeed, if she were to greet my gesture with friendly approval, it could be construed, under the "rules" governing such transactions, as an invitation on her part to establish a new relationship of such intimacy that fannypatting would fall within the unspoken rules applicable to such relationships.

Similarly, unspoken rules may be inferred from behaviors within a family. If, in working with a family, I see the wife crying but the other family members not looking at her, and if, when I ask what her tears are about, she replies, "Nothing," I would infer that an unspoken rule in that family is, "Don't talk about deep feelings." The rule might even be, "Don't *have* deep feelings."

Some commonly encountered rules in families are as follows.

(1) Hostile feelings may (or may not) be expressed.

(2) Try harder; never be satisfied with what you (or anybody else) have done.

(3) Certain tasks are (or are not) men's work, and others are (or are not) women's work.

(4) Discipline (or punishment) is the task of the father (or mother).

(5) Father (or mother, or nobody) is the head of the family.

(6) A college education (or books, or music, or whatever) is highly valued (or not) in this family.

(7) Tidiness is (or is not) highly valued when guests (or mother, or mother-in-law) are expected (or at all times).

The above are only a few of the many unspoken rules that people follow in human systems, often without being aware of them as rules. One function of the family therapist is to make some of these rules explicit, so that the family members may be aware of them and of their effects. Often when a rule is identified, one or more family members may choose to repeal or modify the rule or, on the other hand, to strengthen it. Identifying the rule enables family members to become *aware* that they can choose to keep, modify, or terminate the rule. Recognizing these options and acting on them generally improves the family interaction and the self-esteem of its members.

A dramatic effect of unspoken rules has been observed in families in which a son or daughter is identified as schizophrenic. Such a person is generally regarded by his or her family and physician as being "out of touch with reality." I see the person as being in touch with reality, but it is not the same reality as that of the physician and other family members. In such families, one or both parents typically subject the identified patient to "double binds," that is, no-win situations. The schizophrenic patients studied perceived their home situation to be one in which they were repeatedly subjected to double binds and to the impossibility of winning. Seeing no way to win, or to make sense or order out of the world as presented to them by the double-binding parent, these patients escaped the intolerable situation by creating a separate and more tolerable reality for themselves.

In these studies, however, an apparently simple remedy was found. The remedy was simply to comment on the double bind. To become a winner instead of a loser, the patient had only to open his or her mouth and say, "Mom (or Dad), I don't see how I can win in this situation," or

"This feels like a double bind to me," or words to that effect. When the patient undertook to make that kind of process comment, he or she apparently experienced no further need to withdraw into a separate reality. The significant difference introduced by this process comment appears to be that it identifies and challenges an unspoken rule in the family. That rule was, "We must not comment on the double-bind process," or "We must not comment on the feeling of being helplessly trapped by the options presented to us," or "We must limit ourselves to the options presented to us by this parent." When that rule is eliminated, the crazy-making effect of the double binds is eliminated.

I do not mean that all, or even most, unspoken rules are poisonous in their effect. Many unspoken rules contribute to the self-esteem of family members and to the functional working of the family itself. Some positive rules are: do not rip off one another's personal possessions; we care about the feelings of other family members; we are expected to do what we have agreed to do; meriting the trust of other family members is important. It would probably consume more time than it is worth to identify all unspoken family rules, even if we could do so. But when the family is in pain, when its members are suffering from some dysfunction in the system, it's important to look at the family interaction to see what rules are in operation, what effects those rules are having, and what other rules might be adopted to produce the gratifications that the family members desire.

In addition to the implicit rules discussed above, most families develop a fabric of explicit rules, e.g.: whether and what kind of notice is to be given when a family member is to arrive home later than expected; who is to prepare the meals; who keeps the checkbook and other financial records; who does household chores, such as dishwashing, lawn mowing, trash carrying and the like; what time lights are to go out at night; and what criteria are to be used in selecting television programs, if any.

Families use a variety of methods for establishing these rules. In some families, Father (or Mother) decides, and that's it. In some families, Mother (or Father) decides after consulting the other parent. In some families, the adult partners come to a decision together. In still other families, all family members who are to be affected by the decisions participate in formulating them.

One method of making family rules has been labeled "authoritarian." If I am the rule maker in an authoritarian system, I count myself in, and I count you out. At the opposite extreme is a permissive system. In a permissive system I count you in, and I count myself out. In my experience, both the authoritarian system and the permissive system breed dysfunctional interactions. The person or persons counted out tend to feel resentful and rebellious or, at the other extreme, wind up with such low self-esteem that their habitual posture in life is submissive, placating, despairing, and depressed. I much prefer participative decision making and shared responsibility for generating and maintaining family rules. The family meeting is to me an attractive option.

Family Participation and Family Meetings

At what age can a child be brought into participating in family rule making? In some ways a child may be said to be involved in family rule making from the moment of its birth. The parents listen to the newborn infant's sounds, watch its movements, and try to decode these messages to know what the child is expressing by them. In return, parents communicate unspoken rules to the child, such as: when you cry in the night, we will come in and feed and change you; when we bathe you, we will communicate that we care about you and want you to be comfortable and to enjoy even daily routine experiences; in this family the touching of skin to skin is permitted, and we can enjoy our bodies; you can trust us not to exploit or violate or neglect you in touching.

Usually, very young children do not participate in the making or enforcement of explicit rules. Examples of these rules are: the clothing in my drawers is not to be pulled out and strewn on the floor; you are not to touch the breakable items on this table.

Very soon, however, a child is able to participate in family deliberations at some level. Some children may not be able to respond very effectively to the question, "What shall we have for supper tonight?" However, they might take part very competently in responding to the question, "Should we have hamburgers or hot dogs tonight?" In taking part in deciding such issues, these children are doing more than simply entering into the decision apparently called for by the question; they are having and reinforcing the experience of taking part in the processes of a human system. They are also getting a message vital to their self-esteem: you are loved; you are lovable; you are a valued member of this family; you make a difference; there is a place here for you even when you are not here to fill the place.

There is a practical reason for bringing children into the family's rule-making process as soon as possible: children, like people of all ages, adhere better to rules they have had a hand in making. We all comply better with rules to which we feel committed than we do with rules that are imposed on us. A family meeting is a way to assure that rules will be ones that all family members can accept, and that commitment will be given before the rule is put into effect.

Kinds of Family Meetings

Most family meetings are of two kinds: meetings called to make decisions, solve problems, or resolve conflicts; and meetings for maintenance, which may sometimes take on the character of a family ritual.

Maintenance Meetings: Family Ritual

Some families have meetings more or less regularly. Different families, and different family members, describe the purposes of these meetings in different ways:

— "It's a nice way to have a special time for the family to get together."
— "It's a way to catch up on what various family members are doing."
— "It gives us a chance to see whether our decisions are working out okay."
— "It's a time for focusing on one another in ways that we sometimes forget about during the rest of the week."

However the overt functions of regular meetings are described, they seem to serve two purposes: declaring the importance of all family members; and providing a forum for working out actual or potential conflict situations in the family.

Not all families find ritual or maintenance meetings useful and congenial. Some describe them variously as a drag, a bore, a rehash of old complaints, etc. Those families might do well to consider changing the format or focus of family meetings, or not to have family meetings at all. Even those families, however, will need to have occasional meetings for making decisions and for working out problems that affect some or all of the family members.

Problem-Solving Meetings

The problem-solving or decision-making meeting is, in a way, an extension of the no-lose problem-solving principles and methods discussed in Chapters 7 to 9, with the addition of some considerations derived from the dynamics of group processes generally.

Chapter 7 discusses preliminary steps leading up to the resolution of conflicts betwen two persons. Family members may find these preliminary steps useful when approaching family meetings, particularly when the meetings are intended to resolve conflicts or when conflicts are likely to arise during the course of the meeting. For instance, the first preliminary step discussed in Chapter 7 is, "Who owns the problem?" If sons John and Ned are having trouble deciding on a fair division of the garden chores that they have agreed to do, I as their father may need to keep in mind that I do not own the problem as long as the chores get done; the problem is between John and Ned. If their dispute arises during the family meeting, my role is not that of antagonist or solution finder, but may—if it is acceptable to them—be that of a facilitator in helping them clarify and resolve their problem.

Another question discussed in Chapter 7 is, "Can I fight fairly?" The rules for fighting fairly are discussed at length in Chapter 8, and are worth review if one can guess that a conflict may arise during the course of the family meeting.

Chapter 9 enumerates and discusses the six steps that constitute the no-loss problem-solving method found useful for any two persons involved in a conflict. The same steps are useful for groups of three or more, but some differences in application do arise for such groups.

1. Defining the problem. The first step in defining the problem in conflicts between two individuals is for the aggrieved person to send an I-message to the person whose behavior constitutes the problem. The same opening device is recommended for introducing a problem in a family meeting. One difference may be, however, that the troublesome behavior may be that of more than one person. If so, the Sender may anticipate more than one defensive response. To be effective, then, the Sender would have to consider giving active listening attention to more than one family member; but it is inherently difficult and not very effective to divide one's attention between two people in this way. The Sender might be better able to handle the situation by first getting an agreement that he or she need respond to only one family member at a time. If a family member whose behavior constitutes the problem responds non-defensively, it would be a good tactic to give attention to him or her first, before responding to a defensive family member, since the more positive attitudes will provide a more congenial environment for hearing and accepting the I-message.

A special problem exists if a family member whose behavior is *not* part of the problem nevertheless responds by taking sides either for or against the Sender. In that case, I almost always find it important and effective to address that family member first, to make it clear that his or her behavior is not part of the problem, and that his or her participation in the discussion will therefore be welcome only if it takes the form of facilitation or consultation. (The role of consultant or facilitator is discussed later in this chapter.)

If the I-message is addressed to the family as a whole, or to all members of the family who are taking part in the meeting, then each has a legitimate interst in responding to the Sender. Even in this situation, a family member can still act as consultant or facilitator in an exchange between any two or more other family members (subject to the rules for consultancy and facilitation).

2. Brainstorming. As noted in Chapter 9, brainstorming is an uncritical process that takes place when all disputants have agreed on the definition of the problem. Since it is uncritical, many families have found it acceptable, and often useful, to include all the family members in the brainstorming process, even when the problem itself is of immediate concern to only some of the family members.

Nonparticipation in the brainstorming process by any family member who is a party to the problem is an ambiguous message. The silence may mean acquiescence to what is going on, or it may mean dissatisfaction or disgruntlement. A solution reached without the acquiescence of a party to the conflict will probably not be very effective for very long. It may therefore be important for the Sender of the I-message to feed back how the message of silence is being received and interpreted, and to check out the true meaning of the silence.

3. Evaluating. Although the brainstorming process may well include all family members, usually only parties to the dispute should take part in evaluating the list of solutions developed by the brainstorming process. Here again, it is desirable to check out the meaning of any nonparticipation or silence noticed among parties to the dispute.

4. Choosing. It is important that a solution to the problem be chosen by consensus. There are other ways, but none of them seem to work as well as consensus.

One other way is to flip a coin or otherwise leave the matter to chance. This usually leaves the parties equally disgruntled with the result, and worsens their feelings toward one another.

The effect of leaving the decision to a third party is similar. A solution in terms of content is reached, but somebody is almost sure to feel like a loser in the relationship; so the stage will be set for a series of win-lose confrontations that will undermine and defeat the solution apparently arrived at.

In authoritarian families, rules made by the authority figure are like those made by judges or arbiters. In such families, not only do the imposed solutions tend to come unstuck, but the authority figure also sets in motion feelings of resentment, fear, rebellion, or passive-aggressive behavior.

Majority vote is equated in the minds of many Americans with democratic procedure. The trouble with resolving disputes by majority vote is—unless the vote is unanimous—that there are one or more losers. There may be no overt dissent, since our tacit rules label a person a poor sport if he or she does not go along with the solution arrived at "democratically," but the sense of being a loser is there nonetheless. And it is natural and expectable for losers to feel resentment and to find lots of reasons for being less than wholly committed to the results.

Compromise as a no-lose problem-solving method contains some pitfalls. One risk is that all participants may emerge equally unhappy with the result. Another is that one (or more) of the participants may wind up feeling like a loser. Either result is a sign that, in their zeal to resolve the *content* of the conflict, the disputants have neglected to check out their feelings about the *relationship*.

Unanimity has the happy effect of leaving no losers to challenge or defeat the chosen solution. It has the disadvantage, however, of being impossible to get as long as any family member remains convinced that a different solution would be better.

What to do? Consensus is a way to secure the commitment of all family members to the chosen solution, even when one or more of them are not convinced that the chosen solution is superior to all others. It is a solution arrived at for the sake of the relationship when there is an impasse in terms of the content. I can commit myself to the chosen solution even when I am convinced that it is not the best solution. I can feel myself a winner in doing so because I have chosen happily to take my stand alongside other family members in a solution they have chosen, not because I would have chosen that solution, but because I value and wish to support the commitment to their solution that other family members apparently value. When this kind of consensus is achieved, a kind of joy and release, relief and energy can be observed in families. The effect strengthens the relationship.

5. Implementing. The process of putting the chosen solution into effect is more or less the same in a family meeting as it is in a conflict between two persons.

6. Reviewing and reevaluating. The same may be said for the process of keeping the chosen solution under constant review and reevaluation. The important principle here is that, if there is a breach of the agreement, the family member adversely affected by that behavior can choose either to make the other person wrong (i.e., treat the objectionable behavior as a sin or crime) or to shape the transaction so that both or all parties can come out as winners (i.e., regard the infraction as a new problem to be resolved by the six-point, no-lose problem-solving method).

Consultancy and Facilitation

Family members who are not directly engaged in a conflict that arises during a family meeting may nevertheless play important roles as consultants and facilitators. Essentially this is the same function as that performed by a concerned parent during a conflict between two of his or her children. Briefly, a consultant/facilitator performs the following functions.

A. Intervenes only with the consent of the disputants (but may offer to facilitate).

B. Clarifies communication by: (1) active listening or paraphrasing the message(s) of the disputants, particularly when a disputant seems not to be hearing the message sent; (2) offering his or her own perception of the message being sent, and clearly labeling these interventions as being his or her own perceptions; (3) calling attention to any use of Communication Stoppers (see Chapter 5).

C. Makes process observations about the communication. For example: "Joe, you haven't said whether you are for or against Jerry's suggestion." "Jenny, I hear Jill saying that she doesn't feel heard by you." "Jack, while you've been giving your views, I've noticed the other family members squirming." "Jay, I see tears in your eyes. What's going on?" "Jed, I hear you expressing what you assume to be the feelings of other family members, and I wonder how they feel about that."

D. Makes process observations about the problem-solving sequence. Many disputes about what is to be done take place before the problem is fully identified and defined. In defining the problem, many disputants neglect to give adequate weight to the feelings of all concerned and to the relative importance that each attaches to the content and the relationship. The facilitator can voice his or her perception that the problem-definition step has not been completed.

E. Keeps focus on here-and-now opportunities for solution, rather than on back-then disputes about who did what to whom: (1) translates "the problem is" into "the change I want"; (2) shares his or her own perceptions, and invites perceptions of others about the existence or nonexistence of other options.

F. Gives unconditional positive regard to all disputants, communicating by her or his attitude, focus, and attention that the facilitator's values, sets, and judgments are the facilitator's own, and will not color or dilute the facilitator's impartiality; and communicates also his or her confidence that the disputants have the wisdom ultimately to work out their problems.

G. On occasion, shares his or her own experience when it appears that this experience might supplement the experience of the disputants, and clearly labels these interventions as his or her own experience.

H. Refrains from expressing judgments, giving advice, or using the Communication Stoppers discussed in Chapter 5.

PART FOUR

Particular Problems

11

Value Conflicts

IF YOUR SMOKING bothers me, that is one kind of problem in an intimate relationship. If your religion bothers me, that is an entirely different kind of problem. The six-point problem-solving technique discussed in Chapter 9 may work beautifully if your smoking bothers me, but not at all if your religion bothers me. You may be perfectly willing to brainstorm all kinds of modifications in your behavior so that we can both win on the issue of your smoking. However, you're very likely to consider your religion to be so integral a part of yourself that my rejection of your religion would feel to you like a rejection of yourself.

Sometimes it is hard to know when we are in a value conflict. A common example of this difficulty is the conflict growing out of a parent's insistence that a child keep a neater, more orderly room. It is easy for the parent to say truthfully that the child's behavior is a problem to the parent. But, on examination, it is apparent that the problem presented by the child's behavior is based on a conflict over the value of a neat, orderly room, and over purely subjective judgments about what constitutes a neat, orderly room.

One way to test whether the conflict is a value conflict is to go back to the four parts of the I-message outlined in Chapter 9:

(1) When I see (hear) . . . (briefly describing the offensive behavior),
(2) The practical effects on me are . . .

(3) I feel . . .

(4) I want . . . (briefly describing the behavior change desired).

In the typical value conflict, practical effects on the Sender are difficult (or impossible) to find; e.g., your religion, the length of your hair, your taste in clothes, or your political party affiliations don't have any practical effects on me. So when my behavior is a problem to you, it may well be that you and I are in conflict over values.

If there are no practical effects, do you have no right to express the problem to me, or is there something wrong with you in experiencing my behavior as offensive? Not at all. Feelings about the behavior of another, in any relationship, are relevant to that relationship. The more intimate the relationship is, the more vital is the expression and recognition of that relevance. The crucial difference, however, between value conflicts and those described in Chapter 9 is that "counting myself in" is done quite differently in the two situations. In each situation I want to count myself in, and I want to count you in too. When your behavior has practical consequences on me, however, counting myself in means getting a change in your behavior, or changing the situation, or somehow changing my attitude toward the offensive behavior. In a value conflict, on the other hand, counting myself in does not include demanding that you change your value, since that would amount to my counting you out. In the value conflict, counting myself in consists only of my letting you know how I perceive the conflict and what feelings about it I am owning.

"Owning" is the key word. I want to let you know, because I value you in the relationship, that your religious values, for example, are offensive to me. I want to make it clear, if this is true for me, that this is not a negative judgment of you or of your value to me in this relationship. Rather, I value you enough that I want to let you know what I feel about this difference in our values, because that information about me expresses the kind of openness on which intimate relationships depend. I am letting you know about my negative feelings at some risk. Revealing them to you may result in your rejection of me, a result that I don't want. So in expressing these negative feelings that come up because of our difference in values, I want you to see clearly that I am telling you about myself, and that, in doing so, I am vulnerable to you.

Making Room for the Difference

Let's look at a dialog between a father and his fifteen-year-old son defining a conflict over values.

Father: You're not going to the fathers' and sons' dinner dressed like that, are you?

Son: Sure, why not?

Father: Blue jeans, and no necktie at a banquet?

Son: Sure, what's wrong with that?

Father: What's wrong with it is, when you go to a banquet, you dress for a banquet.

Son: But Dad, all the kids dress like this. If I wore a tie and a suit, they'd think I was a freak.

Father: If I let my son go to a banquet looking like a tramp, the other fathers are going to think I don't know how to bring up a socially responsible son.

You may or may not consider this particular issue important or even interesting. Issues closer to your boiling point may be whether your children use "swear" words, whether your wife wears a "revealing" gown, whether your husband tells "off-color" stories at a party, whether your children's rooms are "tidy," whether your spouse joins with you in some deeply held political conviction, whether your children attend church or synagog, whether your spouse is a "feminist" or "sexist," or what racial attitudes are expressed by various family members, to mention only a few possible value differences. Whatever the conflict, how can it be resolved in a way that will enhance the self-esteem of each of the parties to the conflict, so that each person comes out feeling like a winner? The answer is, as before, by focusing on process rather than on content.

If the disputants cannot resolve their differences in terms of content, they have many opportunities to resolve their differences in terms of process. Usually, the part of process most promising for the resolution of value conflicts is the relationship itself. When you and I are engaged in a conflict over values, we are, at the same time, defining our relationship and the way each of us feels about the relationship. We are influencing whether the relationship feels to us like a place where we must be constantly on guard against intrusions into the integrity of our values, or like a safe and nurturing place in which there is room for both persons and their diverse attitudes and convictions.

Let's see how this approach might be used to resolve the impasse between father and son about how the fifteen-year-old son is to dress for the fathers' and sons' banquet:

Father (making a process comment): We seem to be stuck.

Son (defensively): Well, gee, Dad, I don't want to be the only one there dressed up like a circus horse.

Father (active listening): Being the only one dressed up would be embarrassing to you?

Son: Yes.

Father: So that's where we're stuck. Being overdressed would be embarrassing to you. If you were the only one dressed this casually, that would be embarrassing to me.

Son: Well, I don't want you to be embarrassed, but I'd rather not go at all than to go dressed like for a funeral.

Father: So the choices for you seem to be, to go dressed the way you are, or not to go at all?

Son: Right.

Father: Sounds like not much room in the relationship right now for you to make any change in that for me.

Son: Well, gee, Dad, I hear what you say about being embarrassed, but if I dress up to spare you embarrassment, I feel as though I'm just being used by you.

Father: As though my persuading you to dress according to my values exploits you somehow and doesn't take account of your feelings.

Son: That's right.

Father: So how can we both come out feeling like winners in this situation?

Son: I don't know. Would it help if I wore some better slacks instead of blue jeans?

Father: That sounds good to me.

Son: And maybe a sport shirt instead of a T shirt?

Father: I would like that. But what feels especially good to me is your offering to do that because you value me.

Son: I do, Dad.

Father: So let's forget about the necktie and other formal stuff.

Son: Thanks, Dad, that feels good to me.

In this dialog, the father's active listening reduced the son's defensiveness. The son, in turn, cared enough to make some concessions, and to make it clear that these concessions arose out of his concern for his father's feelings.

It's possible to look on the above as a compromise solution. I think of compromise, however, as each person giving up something in order to arrive at a solution in which everybody comes out feeling like a partial loser. What I look for in resolving a family conflict is a solution in which everybody comes out feeling like a winner. The winning takes place not in terms of content (what the conflict was *about*), but in terms of the relationship. To win in terms of the relationship, the disputants brainstorm, and eventually choose, modifications of their original positions in order to come out feeling enriched and strengthened in the relationship.

If one or more parties to the conflict are not motivated to make a gesture on behalf of the relationship, the effect is to call the relationship itself into question. The implied message may be, "I don't care enough about this relationship to make any concessions in order to preserve it." If that is the issue, it is usually desirable to confront the question expressly and openly.

Content/Relationship Solutions

Not all value conflicts can be solved simply by making room in the relationship for the difference to exist. If I want to live in the country, but my partner is city-bound, it is seldom enough simply to recognize and accept this difference. The difference in value is likely to affect choices that must be made about where to live, what kind of house to live in, how to furnish it, what friends to mingle with, and how to occupy our time.

Similarly, if I place a high value on a large family with many children, but my partner places equally high value on having few children or none at all, the resolution of our conflict is going to require more than our simply recognizing that we have a difference in values. This difference is going to require one or both of us to yield or compromise on how we give practical effect to our differences and values. We are going to have no children, or one child, or two children, or more children, and these choices necessarily entail yielding or compromising one or more strongly held values or dissolving the relationship.

When the issue was whether a teenager was to keep his or her room in a tidy condition to satisfy parental values, or whether the parents could let the teenager be free from requirements about tidiness, we found it relatively easy to make room in the relationship so that both sides could be satisfied without sacrificing or violating dearly held values. In the same way, when partners disagree about politics, each can allow the other to express her or his political convictions without requiring the other to act contrary to conviction. But when the choice is whether to live an urban or a rural life, it seldom seems feasible for one partner to live in the city and the other to live in the country. And when the question is how many children to have, if any, one partner cannot act according to his or her conviction without violating the preference of the other. Here is the ultimate test of what we have been discussing in this chapter: when resolution is impossible in terms of content, it may be possible in terms of the relationshp.

I intend no guarantee that an impasse over content can be resolved for the sake of any relationship. The distinction between content and process is not a magic button. It's merely a way of looking at a conflict, and of reminding the parties to the conflict that the content of the dispute is important to them precisely because the relationship is important to them. It's a way of centering attention on the importance of the relationship, so that primary attention is focused on the desire to strengthen the relationship, rather than on the alienating effects of the content of the dispute.

It may be that principles and values are so dearly held by loving partners that they cannot, in conscience, yield or compromise or even tolerate a difference in the other partner. In that event, the partners may have to face the painful choice of dissolving the relationship or living together with the pain. Short of those extremes, however, is the option of focusing on the relationship, and on the desire of each partner to preserve the relationship. Given that emphasis and that will, partners more often than one might guess can find a solution that is not only acceptable but actually gratifying to both disputants.

Some time ago Marion and I worked with a couple who had shed many tears over an apparently insoluble conflict. The husband was Jewish, and strongly opposed the introduction of a Christmas tree into their home. The wife was Christian, and placed both religious and sentimental value on having a Christmas tree in the house for herself and the children. Marion and I, as consultants, had no suggestions to offer. Instead we role-played the conflict as we were hearing it from the tearful partners. The intensity and genuineness of the couple's feelings about this issue were so strong and so apparent that we had little trouble reproducing, in the roles we had assumed, a similar intensity of feeling and conviction. When we had finished, it was plain to all four of us that we had not arrived at a solution. But the couple seemed somehow a little more at peace with each other, and thanked us for giving them the opportunity to get some distance from the impasse and a slightly different perspective on the problem. A day or so later, we got a joyful phone call. They had found a solution acceptable to both. They had decided to use twigs and branches of fir and holly to make a design on the wall and to decorate them in a manner thoroughly acceptable to the wife and the children. They sounded not only pleased at the resolution of their painful conflict, but actually delighted at the creativity of the answer they had found.

12

Discipline and Punishment

STUDENTS IN OUR CLASSES on "Resolving Family Conflicts So That Everybody Wins" bring up the subject of discipline in two ways: self-discipline and discipline of children. Families who come to me for family therapy or counseling seem to have the same orientation.

Self-Discipline

A typical statement about self-discipline sounds like this: "I've just got to remember to push myself away from the table before I take that second helping," or "I've got to get better control over my temper," or "I'm not very good at disciplining myself to get up at a regular time and go out and look for work."

The message as I hear it is usually a statement by the internal Parent that the internal Child should change. Sometimes, though less often, the statement comes from the internal Adult. (For definitions of the terms Parent, Child, and Adult as used here, see Appendix A.)

When the statement comes from the internal Parent, it is usually self-defeating. The statement implies a message to the Child, "Change," and that implies, "You're not okay." The usual response from the internal Child is like what we could expect from an actual child: a defensive, stubborn, resistant digging in of heels.

When I apply either brakes or the whip to myself, I am not very successful in bringing about the change that I say I want. My experience is that this is also true of most other persons. It's far more effective to pay focused attention to the internal Child—as it is to an actual child—and to bring to bear all the empathy I can muster to discover how the Child's (or child's) behavior makes sense to the Child (or child), and to reaffirm that the person is OK.

Let me illustrate how this works for me. The book you are now reading took me a long time to write. I could have completed it sooner if I had gotten out of bed earlier on the many Saturday mornings that I had set aside for writing the book. I made myself many firm promises to exercise better discipline toward this end, but the firm promises of self-discipline produced no real change in my work pattern until I began to pay some loving attention to what my internal Child was saying. My internal Parent message was, "Come on now, Mendel, you can do better than that." My internal Adult message was, "More hours regularly devoted to the book would speed its completion." But my intractable Child was defeating the process. Clearly I was failing to take into account some need in that internal Child, and the Child was not going to move until I took care of that need.

One effect my internal Child was getting from being intractable was a delay in the completion of the book. Was there a need in me for the result I was getting? That question is often a good starting place when self-discipline is the issue. Sometimes the total organism has a way of bringing about what it really needs. Some of the times in my life when I have come down with colds and fever and have had to go to bed have been at times when I was not paying enough attention to my strong desire to let go of some of my responsibilities and to be taken care of for a while. When I paid attention to that need, lightened my responsibilities somewhat, at least for a while, and asked for more nurturing than I was getting, I had no more need of the cold and fever and could get well again and satisfy my needs in a more adult manner.

In the writing of the book, was there some value to me in postponing its completion? And if there was, what was the value to me in doing it indirectly (by oversleeping, etc.) instead of by making an Adult choice simply to postpone the writing of the book?

I had hardly put the question when an answer began to come clear. I began to become aware of a need to "not know." Writing a book of this kind is a very self-assertive exercise. It implies a lot of knowing.

In writing some of the early portions of this book, I had been plagued by much unexamined self-doubt. Did I really know enough to write the book? Was I generalizing too broadly from what I had read and experienced? Would my experience be adaptable to the lives and situations of persons who might read the book and try to apply it in their lives? In asking those questions, I became aware of an underlying theme that is an old tape for me. This tape says, "Be responsible. Be aware how others may hear your words. Be aware how they may use your words, and what consequences may flow from the way they use them. Be careful. Be considerate." These messages come to me out of my Parent, and I know that I attach great importance to being responsible. I also know, however, that I can burden myself with a responsibility so great and so heavy that it is beyond any real and effective power that I have. Since my internal Parent would not approve of my saying, through my Adult, "I will make my experience available to readers of the book, but I will not be responsible for the way they apply my experience to their lives," my internal Child (bless its heart) found a way to blow the whistle on my excessive self-demands. My Child got tired and needed more sleep and more rest, and couldn't figure out how it wanted to organize the book, and found ways of saying "I can't." Since my Parent refused to permit me to say, "I won't be responsible for how my readers apply my experience," my child protected me from the excessive burden by saying, "I can't get up to write the book. Surely you can't blame me for failing to do what I can't do."

Having given up the burden of excessive responsibility, I found it relatively easy to adopt a more productive schedule for doing the writing I wanted to do.

Self-discipline then became not a matter of more rigorous self-demand, but a more acceptant self-examination.

Discipline of Children

On occasion, after I have attempted to explain the no-lose method of conflict resolution, and particularly after I have stressed the value of making the other person right as well as making myself right (see Chapter 1), I have encountered such questions as, "Don't you believe in discipline at all?"

I value the question because the answer is important. I believe in discipline. I believe in punishment when it is compassionately and pragmatically applied. I believe that physical punishment works against the relationship and undermines the self-esteem of its members.

I think of discipline as a system of rules designed to bring about a willing conformity and loyalty to the authority of the affected group. To me this does not mean training for obedience, subjection, or submissiveness. I observe that authoritarian regimes breed either resentment and resistance, which leads eventually to rebellion and sabotage, or, at the other extreme, defeat, despair, and submissiveness born of fear.

Authoritarian regimes require, for their continuing effectiveness, increasingly stern measures of surveillance and repression. These attributes and effects destroy the very systems they are designed to support, whether those systems be families or nations. I prefer authority to be vested in the members of the group, and rules to be chosen consensually by all those affected, so that each member feels an affirmative interest in the maintenance of the rules and an author's pride in their formulation.

The first step, therefore, in administering an effective system of discipline is to make sure that those who will be bound by the rules have a hand in formulating those rules and feel committed to the maintenance of those rules.

But what shall we do about violations of rules? Most of us have been trained to react automatically: an infraction of a rule is followed by accusation, blame, and punishment. There is evidence from a growing body of research, however, that physical punishment has very little long-range effect on behavior unless the punishment is so severe that most of us would be unwilling to inflict it, and the law would condemn our doing so. The most effective way of bringing about changes in the behavior of rule breakers is to reinforce desired behavior, and to provide as little attention as possible for the rule breaker, who may be seeking just that kind of reward.

I see value in doing something more than ignoring undesirable behavior. I see rule breaking not as a punishable violation of a rule, but as an injury to a valuable relationship existing between the rule breaker and everybody else affected by the misbehavior. I make it clear that the relationship is important to me, and that I value openness, congruence, and authenticity in the relationship. I find it valuable to say that I am hurt and how I am hurt by the infraction, that I cherish the relationship with the rule breaker and those affected by her or his misbehavior, and that I want to work with the rule breaker and other members of the group to repair the damage to the relationship.

I have seen desired changes in behavior flowing from such simple devices as active listening and six-point problem solving, when they are used by persons who feel genuine concern for, and interest in, the rule breaker. The unspoken message in active listening is, "I want to get your message and your meaning in sending the message and the importance you attach to it. I want to see how your behavior makes sense to you. If your behavior is motivated by pain or anger, I want to get a feeling with you of what that pain or anger is like, and how it makes sense to you to act as you have acted under the motivation of that pain or anger." This expression of empathic concern invites the rule breaker to come back and reestasblish his or her place as a valued member of a community to which the misbehavior has relevance. As such it can enhance the rule breaker's self-esteem, and strengthen his or her commitment to the group and its rules.

In summary, I favor discipline, defining discipline to mean training in, conformity to, and respect for a system of rules which all members of the affected group have taken part in formulating and feel a personal commitment to maintain. I do not believe that punishment always contributes to the maintenance of discipline. More effective is the immediate and continued notice and rewarding of desired behaviors, coupled with empathic attempts by members of the community to repair and reestablish a relationship injured by misbehavior.

Punishment

In addition to what I have already said about punishment, I want to make it very clear that I do not always have either the skill or the will to handle rule breaking without resorting to punishment. Sometimes I run out of patience. Sometimes I run out of alternative methods. Sometimes the conditioning I received in growing up directs my actions before I have had a chance to call my later learnings to mind. At those times I may shout, call names, utter threats, impose penalties, and even, on occasion, apply the palm of my hand in anger to a portion of the other person's anatomy. No matter what it is called, this is physical violence as defined in Chapter 8.

Almost instantly after that, I feel guilty. I have failed to live up to my expectations of myself, and I think of the many ways in which I may have done irreversible psychological damage to the other person.

Guilt is a not-OK feeling in my internal Child triggered by critical messages from my internal Parent, saying, "You're bad. You let me down." It takes me awhile to tune in on my internal Parent which says, 'You made a mistake. My expectations of you leave room for the possibility of making mistakes. You will learn from the experience. The victim of your mistake is a separate person, has responsibility for her or his life, and can choose to be injured by what you have done or not." Then my Adult takes over and says, "Now I have two problems instead of one. One is the problem that gave rise to the punishing behavior. That problem remains unresolved. The other is the effect I may have produced on the relationship by my punishing behavior."

The most healing behavior I know of to counteract any negative effects I may have had on the relationship, or on the other person's self-esteem, is our old friend, the process comment (see Chapters 9 and 10), coupled with active listening. For example: "I got very angry, and I hit you. That must have been scary for you, and I am guessing that you are angry with me for doing that. I feel very disapproving of what I did." I do active listening to the answers I get, and I try to make it crystal clear that I respect the other person's feelings, no matter how hostile or rejecting they may be toward me, and that it is safe to express those feelings in any way short of physical retaliation. My principal purpose is to help the other person understand that my punishing behavior is about me, not about the victim of my punishment. In resorting to punishment, I have revealed an aspect of myself that my victim can add to his or her accumulated experience. My behavior is not to be seen as a declaration that the other person is bad, but only that I was angry. It is not to be understood that punishment of the kind I inflicted is to be the rule in this relationship, but only that it was my mode at that time, under that stress.

If there is punishment, let it be punishment that can advance that aspect of the relationship which was injured by the behavior that aroused my punishing response in the first place.

If eleven-year-old Jack has promised to be home from the playground before dark, but does not appear until thirty minutes after dark, a punishment totally unrelated to the offense, such as a spanking or the suspension of a privilege, does not improve the overall situation. A punishment somewhat more related to the offense itself might be a rule against going to the playground for whatever period of time is long enough to impress on Jack the importance of coming home from there on time. A punishment more closely tied to the relationship itself, rather than just to the offensive behavior, might be an agreement between Jack and his mother that the gravest element of his infraction was his lack of concern for her feelings. In that way the relationship itself is brought into focus.

In some families attempts are made to make penalties appear not as punishments, but as consequences flowing naturally from the particular infractions. If Betty misses the school bus because she did not get ready for school on time, she may have to call and take a taxicab to school at her own expense.

Discipline in School or Other Regimented Environments

The disciplinary device of drawing the rule breaker's attention to the relationship rather than imposing penalties, as suggested above, may be difficult and sometimes even impossible in school and other regimented environments.

If I am the teacher of a class of thirty-five hyperactive adolescents who come from homes in areas with high crime rates, I might consider it totally impractical to take one rule breaker aside and devote the time necessary to appeal to her or his interest in the relationship, leaving the rest of the class with reduced supervision. Similarly, in prison situations a guard or other prison official may be dealing with individuals who have had no constructive experience in maintaining trusting relationships.

More and more, however, teachers, probation officers, camp counselors, and even supervisory personnel in detention facilities seem to me to be trying, sometimes successfully, to encourage their charges to participate in the rule making and to share the responsibility for maintaining those rules; and this attempt, no matter how poorly it may work, is itself a valuable experience in forming and maintaining a relationship.

In at least one detention facility for juveniles, there is a room for the confinement of boys whose behavior at the moment is considered detrimental to the group. However, the officers in charge emphasize that the boy is not "sent" there and confined as a punishment; he is persuaded to go there in his own interest and in the interest of the group until he feels himself again able to take his place in the group as a valued member of it. I am aware of the coercive nature of the environment, but I am impressed with the group spirit that flows from the emphasis on "persuasion."

Similarly, in a class of sixth-graders, the teacher, with the principal's help and approval, has discontinued the use of detention after school or in the principal's office for infractions of rules. She has instead set aside a portion of her room, visually separated from the rest of the room by shelves filled with books, playthings, a blanket, a pillow, and a rug, where the misbehaving boy or girl can be temporarily removed from the overstimulating effect of the entire group until he or she appears more able to resume his or her place as a responsible member of the group.

These attempts to turn away from the old methods of punishment are not always successful. They focus new attention on responsible maintenance of group membership, not by lecturing, preaching, guilt, or threat, but by giving evidence that the rule breaker is a valued member of the social group, and by focusing attention on the valued relationship rather than on the behavior alone. As a society, we have had extremely limited experience with these methods. In times to come, our experiments will probably be considered extremely primitive. I am encouraged, however, by the willingness to try and to experiment that I see. And I am additionally encouraged by successes I see flowing from those efforts and experiments, even in the primitive state of our present knowledge.

13

Differences in Desire and Timing, Sexual and Otherwise

WHAT IS TO BE DONE when you desire your partner sexually, but she or he is not "in the mood," or vice versa? The problem is not limited to sexual encounters. It arises in many other situations. I want to go to a movie tonight, but you would rather stay home and read. You have your heart set on a vigorous vacation in the mountains, but I want to lie on the beach.

In resolving most of these differences, the principles discussed in Chapter 11 for resolving value conflicts can be successfully applied. The guiding principle is to resolve the disagreement in terms of the relationship level when there is an impasse over content. That is, when there is enough caring for the other person in the relationship and the will to count both partners in, a solution can generally be found that leaves both partners feeling like winners.

However, finding such a solution when dealing with sexual timing and desire seems more difficult than for almost any other content area. The chief reason for this appears to be that the question of sexual desire and timing are overlaid with a host of myths, feelings, expectations, and attitudes that complicate even the most seemingly simple and innocent communication.

Symbolic Nature of Sexual Encounters

If you say to me "Let's go to bed," and you accompany the invitation with a particularly inviting look, I may start a tape like the following running through my head:

The expression on her face looks like a challenge. I hate challenges. The sexual challenge carries with it, for me, the implication that I might not measure up to some standard of performance expected of me. My Not-OK Child wants to measure up to what is expected of me, but fears that I won't measure up. If I say "Yes" now to the invitation I have received, it will be like trying to jump through hoops. If I say "No," it may be understood as declining the challenge because I fear that I shall fail. Somehow my OK-ness as a male is at stake. I have allowed my OK-ness to get involved with the self-expectation that I measure up to a certain standard of performance. My ideal for performance is to be instantly hard and erect and ready to meet every sexual opportunity, to be experienced by my partner as a superb lover, to be responsible for my partner's pleasure as well as my own, to meet that responsibility with colors flying, to bring us both to orgasm simultaneously, and somehow to be ready for a renewed encounter in a time so short that my partner will be amazed and impressed.

But it is not only the male who has woven into sex a Himalayan confusion of impossible self-expectations. If I am a female confronted with a sexual invitation, I may have several self-images competing for precedence. One may be that of the chaste "good girl," who is surprised when anyone sees her as available sexually. Another may be that of the voluptuous, inviting play-bunny of the centerfold and the theater marquee, who matches any partner in passion and enjoyment. A third self-image is likely to be that of all-nurturing earth mother, always there for her man, ready and delighted to do his bidding, to give him joy, to understand his moods, to accept his failures, to encourage his efforts, to confirm that he has delighted her and deepened her love for him. Or I may be militantly independent, even rejecting. In addition to all these questions about who I am as a woman, I may wonder sometimes whether my partner's invitations to me reflect a desire only for my body or for the gratification of his needs, or whether they are evidence of a genuine love and regard for the essential person I feel myself to be.

With all this confusion of image and expectation, it's small wonder that a difference in desire or timing in the sexual life of intimate partners may be experienced far differently from a difference in desire or timing in any other area. If the question is whether we go to a movie or stay home, the transaction is a relatively simple one of deciding what to do in such a way that we both feel valued as partners in the relationship. If, however, the question is whether to go to bed or not at the invitation of one partner, the transaction consists of far more than what to do. In many ways the transaction is likely to be seen as: Who am I? How competent am I? How adequate am I? Do I dare expose my feelings of inadequacy and self-doubt to this partner who means so much to me? Is the risk of losing this partner greater if I attempt to perform, or if I decline to perform?

The most effective remedy I know to overcome this welter of myth, miscommunication, and confusion is to take the following steps.

1. *Get your own head straight.* Be honest with yourself about who you are, what you want, and what you can do. Accept yourself where you are and make that OK. Take a close look at what shoulds and musts you are putting on yourself, and throw them out. Shoulds and musts get in the way of joyful and satisfying sexual relationships.

2. *Reexamine your assumptions* about what is, or will, or may be expected of you as a sexual partner, and throw those assumptions out. Many men harbor the fear that they will be ridiculed if they fail to obtain or maintain an erection in a sexual encounter with a woman. Perhaps some women who do not know the realities of sex may consider their partner impotent or inadequate if this occurs. But in my experience most women understand that erection is not always a sure thing, and form no adverse judgment of a partner when that very common and expectable event occurs. Women too sometimes assume that their failure to attain orgasm every time will result in adverse judgment. To avoid these negative judgments, some women fake orgasm. Men who understand sexual reality, however, know that orgasm is not always a sure thing either, and are acceptant of this reality when it occurs. Some men, on the contrary, pride themselves on bringing their partners to orgasm, and consider themselves to be failures if they can't satisfy their partners, just as some women whose partners fail to reach orgasm blame themselves for not being attractive enough to keep their mates in a state of perpetual arousal.

Examine your assumptions about what will be expected of you in a particular sexual encounter. Try not to generalize from unexamined assumptions about what "most men" or "most women," or even this particular sexual partner, will want or do or expect.

3. *Be honest.* Be open. Send straight messages. Here are some examples of straight messages.

a. I would like to go to bed with you right now.
b. I am not interested in sex tonight, but I would like you to hold me.
c. I am afraid to ask you to go to bed with me, because I am afraid you will be critical of my lovemaking.
d. I am afraid to ask you to go to bed with me, because I am afraid you will put me down if I don't have a climax with you.
e. I am afraid to make love with you, because I am afraid you will want me to take part in some sexual innovations that I may not want to engage in.
f. I don't want to perform that particular sexual act that you request of me, but I don't want you to hear that as a rejection or criticism of you.
g. I am too tired to have sex with you now, but I would like to do it when I feel rested.
h. I am too angry with you to want sex with you right now. This is not a punishment of you; it is a statement that I am not feeling loving right now.
i. I like the way you are making love with me now.
j. I would like you to stop doing what you are doing in our lovemaking now, but I'm glad you felt safe enough with me to try it.
k. I would like you to do this with me in our lovemaking.

Many couples have developed particular words or signals or gestures that constitute straight communication between the two of them, although others would not understand their private language. The question, "Do you want to have a party?" may be clearly understood by that particular couple as a sexual invitation. For another couple, a playful swat on the rear end may carry the same message. Unless this private language is clearly understood, however, miscommunication may result from failure to use precise language. One wife complained that her husband made overtures to her even when she indicated her lack of desire by turning her back to him in bed. The husband expressed surprise at this complaint during marital counseling, stating that he had never understood his wife's nonverbal gesture to mean that she did not want a sexual encounter. When her meaning was made clear to him, he expressed willingness to comply with her desires.

4. *Prefer relationship to content.* When there is an impasse in the content of a dispute over sexual timing, resolve the conflict in terms of the relationship. The conflict may consist of one partner's desire for sex now, and the other partner's desire not to have it now. For either partner

to win in the content, the other partner would have to lose, and if either partner loses, both lose. But resolution may be possible in terms of the relationship. If I want sex with you now, and you do not want sex with me now, you can help me feel like a winner, even though I do not get to take you to bed right now, by helping me experience some gain or gratification in the relationship. Perhaps I will feel good in the relationship simply because I have an opportunity to show my caring and concern for you by not pressing you to have sex with me when you don't want to. I can feel even better about this if I get immediate recognition and reinforcement from you for having been understanding, compassionate, and considerate in respecting your wishes. Another way for me to feel like a winner in the relationship would be for us to have a clearly understood and comfortably accepted agreement that either of us can ask for sexual intercourse with the other whenever we want it, and that the other will be absolutely straight about saying yes or no, so that we always have the gratification of knowing that we are perpetuating and supporting a healthy, working relationship.

5. *Take the goal orientation out of sex.* Many couples seem to equate sexual satisfaction with orgasm. As a result, they fail to see that all the sexual play preceding and following orgasm has value, joy, pleasure, and delight in itself. When people consider lovemaking just a way to "get there," it has no value to them if they don't "get there." One effect of this goal orientation is anxiety. "Am I going to make it? If I don't make it, the whole experience has been a failure." I would like to suggest another way to experience lovemaking. It is to view the sexual encounter as a second-by-second series of pleasurable stop-action experiences: what I do sexually at this moment is a pleasurable sexual experience valuable in itself; and the next moment is another separate pleasurable sexual experience; and the next moment, and the next moment, and so on. I have no goal; I have only this moment. I have the pleasure and delight of this moment even if the world ends now. I can end the encounter now with no disappointment, whether or not orgasm becomes a part of this series of sexual experiences. What I do in this sexual encounter is what I do. What I do in this sexual encounter is not a test of me or of you; it is simply what I do. If I have orgasm as a part of this sexual experience, I have orgasm. If I have orgasm as a part of this sexual experience, it does not make either me or you a better or worse person; it is simply an experience. If I do not have orgasm as a part of this sexual experience, that is not a test of me or you; it is simply an experience. If I do not have an orgasm as a part of this sexual experience, that is simply an experience that I have; it does not change or spoil

any other part of the sexual experience that I have had. My sexual experiences are unique to me. I have the right sexual experiences for me. Sexual experiences that others have are right for them, but are not a measure of what is right for me. What I like and dislike in sex are just right for me. What others like or dislike in sex cannot be used as measures of what I like or could or should like. What others may expect of me in sex expresses something about them, but is not a measure of anything about me. I can let them have their expectations without taking those expectations on. I can look at their expectations as ways of knowing those persons better, since their expectations are about them, not about me, and are not a guide for me. I may consider their expectations to be options which I may try if I so choose, but not as measures of what is right for me.

Road Map for Communication About Sex

Figure 13.1 is a road map for resolving conflicts over sexual desire and timing. The steps in it are as follows.

The Sender makes a clear statement (verbally or otherwise) about what he or she desires.

The Receiver has an absolute right to say yes or no, or to make a counterproposal, or to request information or clarification or more time. If the answer is yes, no problem.

If the Receiver says no to the invitation, the Sender would do well to check out the precise meaning of the rejection. Does it mean no forever? For just here and now? Would alternatives be welcome? Is the no delivered in a way that makes clear the refuser's concern for the other's feelings in the relationship? If not, what are the implications?

If the Receiver makes a counterproposal, the Sender has an absolute right to say yes or no, to make a counterproposal, or to request information or clarification or more time. If the answer is yes, no problem. If no, the counterproposer would do well to check out the meaning and implications.

If both the proposal and counterproposal(s) have been rejected, the relationship itself may be in trouble, and the partners may need to have some open communications about what is in the way. If either partner will not agree to discuss the situation or will not communicate openly about what is in the way, the viability of the relationship itself is open to question, as it is if the parties do communicate openly, but cannot agree on times, places, and methods that feel good to both.

In my experience, good, caring communication is healing, and may be a turn-on itself.

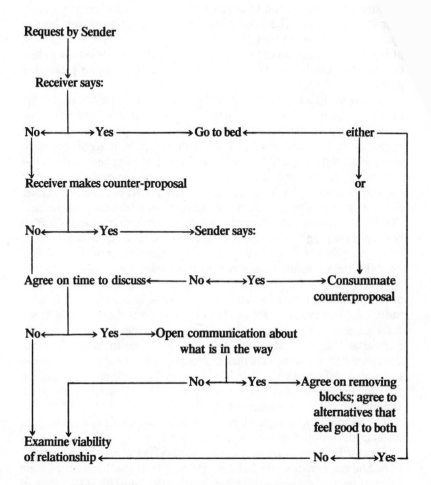

FIGURE 13.1. *Road map for straight communication and resolving conflicts about sex and sexual timing.*

Sex as Communication

When an individual or a couple comes to me for sexual therapy or counseling, the sexual problem is almost always accompanied by problems in communication.

Suppose a couple presents the problem as the man's "impotence" or "premature ejaculation" or as some other specific problem he is having. Sometimes we may treat the symptom directly, but more often

n to suggest corrections in the couple's com-
.e woman may be sending put-down messages to
.ng his self-confidence. She may be demanding more
. ne can deliver. She may be giving so little time to him
unworthy. The list is as various as the couples presenting
.

.rtainly do *not* mean here that the woman's behavior "causes" the
.an's symptoms. The man experiences the woman's behavior as he does because he has been conditioned by all his past experience. He responds to his partner's behavior with attitudes, perceptions, sets, memories, reflexes, and feelings that originated long before she was a part of his life. In a very real sense, he chooses how to experience her. If she complains that his lovemaking is too rough, he can conclude either that she prefers a gentler style, or that he is an inadequate sex partner. He chooses how to experience his partner's behavior, on the basis of all his experience up to that time—much of it accumulated before he even knew her. So she cannot be said to cause any symptom in him. She provides the stimulus. He decides what to make of it.

And he is not the prisoner of his conditioning. He can make new decisions about how to react to his partner's behavior. That is what individual therapy is all about. The sufferer learns that she or he is not the victim of her or his experience or conditioning. If a man hears his partner as blaming and critical just as he perceives his mother, he can conclude that all women are blaming and critical, and that he is helpless to discover how to please them. Or he can make a different decision: the fact that his partner and his mother are both blaming and critical is not a statement about him or his competence.

The woman, too, may have power to affect the man's symptom, even though his conditioning may antedate her by many years. She can let him know in many ways that she has unconditional positive regard for him. She can demonstrate that it is safe for him to trust her with intimate disclosures and openness. She can help him to build his self-esteem in ways discussed in Chapter 1. That she has this power, however, is the cause neither of the man's symptom nor of his "recovery." He is responsible for that. What his partner does is to provide a new, supportive environment for him.

What I have said about sexual dysfunctions in the male partner applies equally to dysfunctions in the female. The couple or individual may present the problem, for example, as the woman's "failure" to achieve orgasm or as her being "turned off" to sex. And we may prescribe activities and homework for the treatment of the symptom directly—usually with success and deep gratification. But more often than not, we find reason to suggest creative attention to the couple's communication pattern. The woman may be complaining that the man never reaches for her except to initiate an encounter for the ejaculatory release of his own sexual tension. Or she may see him as insensitive to her desire for tenderness or for self-fulfillment in a career. Or she may interpret the time he spends at work as a message that she is unattractive or unworthy.

However accurate her descriptions of his behaviors may be, neither partner "causes" the other's symptoms. The woman experiences the man's behavior as she does because she has been conditioned by all her past experiences. She responds to her partner's behavior with attitudes, perceptions, sets, memories, reflexes, and feelings that originated before he was a part of her life. She chooses how to experience him. If he ejaculates before she is satisfied and then rolls over and goes to sleep, she can conclude either that he needs more information about her needs or that she is sexually deficient. If he wants sex more often than she does, she can either see it as a difference in desire and timing between two OK people or choose to consider herself "abnormal."

She is not the slave of her conditioning. She can change from seeing herself as too slow, can learn to recognize that what she experiences about her rhythm and timing is just right for her. She can change from seeing all men as deceitful or insensitive to seeing her mate as an individual with his own qualities and capacities for change.

Just as the woman has power to affect her symptoms, her mate may also have power to affect them, by providing her with behaviors that she can experience as enhancing to her self-esteem and responsive to her needs.

In short, a couple's sexual patterns are parts of the entire fabric of their interactions. Their presenting problem may be differences over money, religion, discipline of children, sex, or chores. But the solution is to be found in terms of the overall quality of their relationship.

14

Compulsive Behavior

WHEN "PROBLEM" DRINKING, gambling, nail-biting, smoking, eating, stealing, or other compulsive behavior is identified as the trouble in the relationship, I expect to find almost always that the underlying problem is one of relatively low self-esteem. For the most part, people with high self-esteem don't drink or gamble compulsively. They drink or gamble when they want to, and they stop drinking or gambling when they want to stop. The same may be said of excessive smoking or eating or almost any compulsive behavior. So when the problem presented is excessive or compulsive behavior, I want to help the troubled family look for ways to enhance the self-esteem of its members.

It is a Family Problem

My bias is that troublesome behavior by one family member is not the problem of that family member alone. The troublesome behavior may itself increase family pain, but it also represents some other kind of family pain that was not originally caused by the problem behavior. Oddly enough, most family systems perpetuate rather than correct the problem behavior. In working with a family that is trying to cope with compulsive behavior in one of its members, I try to encourage all family members to look at the problem as belonging to the family as a whole, rather than as belonging to only the one family member who apparently needs help.

What kind of family problem would not only perpetuate the unwanted behavior, but actually encourage and reinforce it? One common situation is that in which the nondrinking or nongambling partner cherishes the role of nurse or caretaker or protector or martyr. These roles or self-images are seldom conscious, but can often be uncovered, to the satisfaction of all family members, in effective counseling. This is only one example of how unconscious motivations can perpetuate and even encourage a behavior pattern that all family members genuinely want to change.

When families understand that the unwanted behavior is a family problem rather than an individual problem, often there is an almost immediate improvement in the self-esteem of all family members.

As was discussed in Chapter 1, one of the elements that support high self-esteem is the sense of belonging. In undertaking together the project of correcting behavior that is a problem to the family, the family members enrich their sense of being joined in a common project, that is, their sense of belonging. They also improve their sense of competence. Correction of problem behavior that had baffled them now seems at last to be within their reach. And when it is recognized and accepted that problem behavior has its origins in low self-esteem, family members can begin to feel more able to make sense and order out of their world.

Make it Right

One of the family's most effective tasks can be to adopt the "first principle" discussed in Chapter 1: Make both myself and the other person right. This may be an elusive task. When family members learn to do it, however, they often get dramatic results.

How can I make an excessive smoker right, if I perceive her or his behavior as having a painful effect on me? Listen:

Fred: I notice you're smoking again.

Helen: I got so frantic for a smoke that I wasn't sure I could get through the day without it.

Fred: Your doctor said something about emphysema.

Helen: I can't stand your nagging me.

Fred: I don't want to nag you, but I have a stake in this too.

Helen: What is your stake?

Fred: Number one, I love you, and I don't want to lose you.

Helen: If my life were to be like this morning without cigarettes, I wouldn't be much to love—for you and for me both.

Fred: You're saying it's a survival matter to you—not worth surviving unless you can fill that need for a smoke.

Helen: That's exactly what I'm saying.

Fred: So it's a struggle between killing yourself by smoking and kind of a living death if you don't smoke.

Helen: It feels good to me that you bother to know how it is for me.

Fred: And each day—each time you put a cigarette up to your mouth—is a new decision with survival at stake.

Helen: And that struggle seems to be a losing battle, no matter how it comes out. I get depressed.

Fred: I'd like to see you come out a winner.

Helen: So would I.

Fred: How could you do that?

Helen: I don't see any way to do that.

Fred: I'd like to make a suggestion.

Helen: What is it? Just don't nag me.

Fred: I see this as not your problem alone; it's *our* problem.

Helen: *My* disease and *my* smelly habit and *my* powerlessness—you want to cut yourself in on a deal like that?

Fred: I wish we didn't have that problem, but we do. And we are in it together because I choose you—the whole package—emphysema and smells and depression—the whole package.

Helen (cries): It's as though the decision had been made for me when I was little.

Fred: It probably felt like that when you were young.

Helen: Sometimes I can almost hear my father's voice saying, "Once you start you can't stop." I sure make him right, don't I? When can I be right?

Fred: You can make a new decision any time.

Helen: You make it sound so simple.

Fred: I know that new decisions are not always easy, but it's true, isn't it? You can make a new decision.

Helen: If I were in this alone, I would choose cigarettes and an early death.

Fred: And since you're not in this alone . . .?

Helen: I can't deny that we're all in this together. But we're all working against my stubborn little internal Child.

Fred: She's an important part of our decisions.

Helen: When we try to end-run around her, she defeats us all.

Fred: What does she want? Maybe we can make her happy—at least satisfied—and still get what we want.

Helen: We really haven't done much little Child stuff for a long while.

Fred: Nice to remember some impetuous things we've done at the urging of that Child.

Helen: With more sympathetic attention to her, maybe our internal Parent could be stronger.

Fred: For now, though, let's stop sending hate messages to the Child in you. She does what she does because it makes some kind of sense for her to do it.

Building Self-Esteem

Having adopted the basic stance of making us both right, all the affected family members can embark on a program of enhancing and heightening the self-esteem of all family members. I would suggest, as a first step, that you consider relieving yourself of the terrible burden of trying to do better and failing, of then feeling guilty and inadequate, of resolving to try harder and failing again, and so on in a seemingly endless pattern of losing. Losing is not a very good position in which to try to build self-esteem. Winning is a better position. How can you make yourself a winner? Probably the most apparent way of making yourself a winner is to choose to do what you know you can do, and to choose not to do what you know you can't do. I know that I stand five feet, seven inches tall. If I make it my goal at age sixty-two to be six feet tall, I am making myself a loser. Instead, if I choose to be five feet, seven inches tall, I am already a winner.

Similarly, if I continue to make promises to myself that I have made and broken in the past, I am setting myself up to be a loser. And my self-esteem will continue to erode. On the other hand, if I give up making promises that I have repeatedly made and broken in the past, I can make myself a winner by giving it up. I can say to myself, "I have often promised myself to stop with one drink, but I wind up breaking that promise and drinking more than I want to drink, and getting effects in my body and in my family that I don't want. Now I'm going to give up being a loser. I'm going to give up making promises to myself that I know I don't keep. When I promise to stop with one drink, I don't keep that promise to myself. It feels to me that I *can't* keep that promise to myself. One thing I can't do is to be younger than I am. Another thing I can't do is to repeal the law of gravity. Another thing I can't do—or so it seems to me—is to stop after one drink. I'm going to give up trying to do what I apparently can't do. I'm going to be a winner by accepting myself as I am. Now I can look at other options. One option is to drink and not try to stop. Another option is to join Alcoholics Anonymous. Another option is to find out for myself in therapy what need in me I seek to gratify by my pattern, and to look at other ways of gratifying that need."

Using steps such as these, family members can increase their sense of competence, their sense of belonging, and their feeling of being able to make sense and order out of their world. With the growth of self-esteem, compulsive behavior is likely to diminish.

Satisfying the Internal Child

One problem with firm promises to change, and strenuous efforts to give up compulsive behavior, is that the internal Child tends to hear the promise to change as a declaration that "You're not OK." The Child tends to respond defensively and defiantly. This is likely to be the problem with rigorous diets. The overweight person says, "I want to be more slender. I'm going on a diet." The internal Child is likely to hear this and to experience the diet itself as a deprivation. Like real children, the internal Child responds to deprivation with more demands, and also has ways of defeating the whole person unless its demands are met. Soon the dieter finds himself or herself sneaking and nibbling here and there of goodies not on the diet. More successful dieters pay attention to what needs the overeater is trying to satisfy in eating. If overeating is used by the individual as a symbolic or sublimating way to gratify an unmet need for attention or affection or love, it is important first to recognize the unmet need and to find out whether the need is still unmet or whether the feeling of deprivation persists inappropriately from a time when deprivation was experienced as real. As a second step, it is important to pay attention to the present feelings of need for oral satisfaction, whether or not they are based on any real present needs. Since the feelings themselves are real, whether or not there is now any actual deprivation, let us pay attention to the pain that persists from those old feelings of love hunger, and do something for our internal Child, so that it will not insist on our overeating.

One way to take care of the Child might be to provide it with more genuine expressions of affection, attention, and importance. Another might be to provide it with some substitute gratification, such as an occasional chocolate sundae, or something extravagant to wear, or an evening of dancing, or whatever is likely to be perceived by the Child as a step toward gratifying that gnawing hunger for love and attention.

The same holds for stealing or drinking or gambling or other compulsive behavior. Pay attention to the behavior as evidence of the internal Child's demands. Give validity to the demands as based on the little person's perception of what was required to survive. Take steps to gratify the demands in acceptable ways, so that the Child will not dig in its heels and defeat our purposes. When a real child makes true for

himself or herself the messages sent by parent figures that the child is
OK, the child can give up obstreperous and defiant and manipulating
behavior, and is likely to be experienced by others as delightful and
cooperative. So it is also with the internal Child.

The Disease Theory

It is widely but not universally held, among alcoholics and among
persons interested in the welfare of alcoholics, that alcoholism is a
disease. The disease theory has gone far toward reducing the destructive view that alcoholics were criminals, morally bad, or somehow
mentally deficient. Many alcoholics adopted these destructive views
about themselves, and suffered agonies of shame and guilt and despair
as a result. The disease theory of alcoholism has helped many alcoholics give up their heavy burden, acknowledge their predicament, and
seek help.

Under the disease theory, alcoholics are often urged never again to
take another drink. This view is held even among many "alcoholics"
themselves. Others assert that if alcoholism is a disease, it is a curable
disease, and is a disease only in the sense that any compulsive behavior
is a disease, such as compulsive gambling, compulsive smoking,
compulsive eating, compulsive talking, compulsive nail-biting, or
compulsive stammering, is also a disease. My own bias in counseling
clients is to assure them that I respect their power to attain the objectives
that they want in their lives. I consider them to have made choices in
their lives which at the time made sense and order in the world, and
contributed to their survival as they then saw it. Many of those choices
are no longer remembered. Nevertheless, they can be reviewed and
remade or unmade, whenever the client is ready to reexamine his
perceptions of the world and to make new decisions. I don't at all
discount the difficulty and pain of reexamining and remaking these old
decisions, and I don't look down on people who elect not to incur that
difficulty and pain. I do, however, share in the joy, elation, and relief of
those who have dared and succeeded.

15

Parent-Teenager Conflicts

AMONG THE MOST BITTER and intractable conflicts are those between parents and teenagers. Some of these are marked by bitter words on one or both sides, some by hostile silence on one or both sides. In all these conflicts I see heart-wrenching pain.

A more subtle and elusive but equally painful pattern between parents and teenagers is that in which the teenager has given up the fight and has become passive, submissive, fearful, placating, sometimes depressed, and sometimes suicidal.

If you are a teenager, often embroiled in angry disputes with one or both of your parents, try saying *to yourself:* "You can't make me." Say it softly enough so that you won't be heard by anybody except maybe your dog or your cat: "You can't make me." Just that, for now. Say it to yourself over and over until you feel comfortable with it: "You can't make me."

"Let me turn to the parents who may be engaged in angry disputes with teenagers. Parents, notice that I have suggested to your teenagers that they practice saying, "You can't make me." Now I want to suggest that you practice saying, "I can't make you." Don't say it loud enough for other family members to hear it. Not just yet. We'll say it loud enough a little later: "I can't make you."

In saying "You can't make me" or "I can't make you," you are not taking a moral position or acting out something loaded with shoulds or rights or wrongs; you are simply saying, "I recognize that this is the way things are in the part of the universe in which I live." The way things are is that, if I am a teenager, the parent figures in my life can't make me. If I am a parental figure in the lives of teenagers with whom I am in conflict, I can't make them.

It is also true that, if I am a teenager, I can't make them (adults) do anything. And if I am a parental figure, they can't make me.

When families recognize the truth of what I am saying here—that they can't make other family members do anything—I sometimes see them break out into laughter. It is so simple. they have been quarreling and arguing for nothing. One 16-year-old said with great surprise, "I had it all the time, didn't I? I didn't need to fight for it: I had it all the time!" He laughed.

What is it that he had? I like to call it power. Let's look at how it works.

Power

I am Peter's father. Under other circumstances, I might be Peter's stepfather, or maybe his camp counselor, or his boss on the job. Make it anybody occupying a parental position in relation to Peter. At another time or with another individual the content of a message might be about overspending allowance, speeding, violating curfew. That doesn't matter; we are not looking now at the *content* of the message. We are looking at the *process*.

Mendel: I notice you got another citation from the police.

Peter (Remains silent. Doesn't look up from his book.)

Mendel: I told you that you would be grounded if you got one more citation.

Peter (Gets up, starts for door.)

Mendel: Where are you going?

Peter (No answer.)

Mendel: You're not going out of this house until we settle this.

Peter (Stops, turns around, gives father a silent look full of anger. Takes keys out, throws them in the air, catches them, turns and goes out.)

Mendel: Come back here. (Sound of door closing, car being driven off.)*

In this dialog, I see Peter as exercising power. He is saying nonverbally, "You can't make me." The father feels challenged. He thinks about how he can exert more pressure, more persuasion, more coercion. Peter thinks about how to blunt his father's efforts. They will both lose.

When Peter was little, the father's pressures were more successful. In those days, Peter perceived withdrawal of parental approval as a threat to survival. This may never have been expressed in words, but at some level the little person accepted his utter dependence on the parent figures.

The parent figures also take it for granted that a command to young children *will* be obeyed—almost as though any other outcome is unthinkable.

Well, that doesn't work for teenagers. The kids have become accustomed to commands and obedience, but they are breaking away from the unexamined assumption that commands must automatically be obeyed. They are questioning those assumptions.

We taught them to question their assumptions, to have independent minds. In a number of ways, they have tested the rule that parental commands must be obeyed and that we won't stand for anything less than obedience.

Too many families then try coercion. Commands having been proven inadequate and insufficient, the parent figure often tries pressure.

Sometimes coercion works—in a way. But it works only in the short run and at considerable cost to the relationship.

So, back to Power. You have been saying to yourself, "You can't make me; I can't make you." This might feel like giving up power. Not so. It is giving up an old perception that no longer works for you. If commands don't work, what is left? Whatever we try will be subjected to testing, scrutiny, and criticism, a trait we would do well to cultivate and encourage.

Now and then parents and teenagers unite in pretending that the parent figures can still "make" the other person do something. Not so. I see the teenager's "No" as a healthy assertion that the child has completed one part of her or his development and is going on to the next, as part of the process of leaving the nest, but not all at once. On the teenager's side, it is a way to pretend that the parent figures won't "let" the kids do something, that the rule-making and enforcing power is still with the parent figures. Try it for yourself: You be the teenager; I'll be the parent.

Teenager: The party is going to be unchaperoned.

Parent: I can't accept that at all.

Teen: I hear that you don't approve, but I am not asking for your approval.

Parent: It sounds as if you are defying me.

Teen: I don't intend to defy you, but I would like you to see that we can both win only if neither expects the other to knuckle under and be a loser.

Parent: All right, let's try. Here is my value. I consider an unchaperoned party for kids your age to be inviting trouble.

Teen: These are good kids. You have met them all. Lots of them go to unchaperoned parties.

Parent: I'm hearing now that you and I are tangled in reasons and reasons and reasons. Our usual experience with these debates is that neither one is persuaded, frustration builds, anger follows.

Teen: Well, gee . . .

Parent: Let's get off the content and stay in the process. I want to hear how important this is to you. And I want you to hear how important it is to me.

Teen: All right. I would like you to hear that on a scale of one to ten, my interest in the party is about a four.

Parent: As for me . . .

Teen: Just a minute. I also want you to hear this. My preference may be only a four for this particular party, but it is pretty close to ten on the subject of your authority. I fight your rule making, even though I am sometimes privately glad I can say to the other kids, "My Dad won't let me."

Parent: I'm hearing you say that you might cooperate with some rules more readily if I didn't hassle you quite so much with my strict Parent.

Teen: That's true.

Parent: I think I can do that. I could welcome your taking part in forming some of our rules and pointing out to me how I waste power in our discussions. Now I would like to brainstorm the subject of adequate supervision without spoiling your fun and my relief.

Relationship

Along with the teenager's growing will to experiment with a new sense of power and of ability to survive is a growing pattern of experimentation with relationships and with the fundamental question, "Who am I in relationships?" Not only are the healthy teenagers increasingly attracted to relationships with other young people; they are also making a fresh appraisal of parental ways of relating, primarily in terms of how these ways affect them, but also in terms of adopting or rejecting these patterns of relating as they contemplate moving into significant relationships of their own choosing. It's not easy for many parents to hear the negative judgments passed upon them by their teenagers during this process of appraisal, but the reviewing and reappraising is essential for the adult that the teenager is becoming.

For the parents of these "fractious," "bewildering," "rebellious" (or withdrawn) teenagers, it's all very well to step back and try to understand that the disturbing behaviors of their teenagers grow out of perfectly normal and even desirable drives. But it hurts. Rejection by anybody is bad enough. Rejection by one's own cherished offspring is doubly bad, and the hurt is likely to be compounded by the fact that the teenager may question and reject not only the parents' ways of relating with the critical teenager, but also the parents' entire value system and fundamental character.

At the same time, the teenager's growing separation, and sometimes alienation, from the home of origin amounts to a rejection of the parent's parenting function, by which the parent may have been defining himself or herself. It also arouses deep and often well-grounded fears for the physical and social safety of the young experimenter.

Pain and Power

One element common to both sides in a conflict between parents and teenagers is the pain that both feel. And the pain seems to be intensified by the fact that each feels powerless to make itself heard or understood by the other. My perception of parent-teenager conflicts with which I have worked is that both sides throw away much of their power and so keep themselves locked in an abrasive struggle which, for some, is never resolved.

Teenagers throw away power by insisting that the parents change or yield first. This is a part of their childhood pattern, from which they have not yet emerged. Blaming is a way of remaining dependent. As long as reconciliation depends on the parents' making the first move, the teenager has not taken on responsibility for the situation and the outcome. It's a kind of hidden, transitional way of continuing a part of the dependency pattern of childhood while experimenting with letting go. Although this tactic is understandable, it keeps the teenager from exercising the power implicit in daring to take the first step to resolve the confrontation and to reduce the pain.

Parents have many types of power in such struggles. They have the power to encourage the exercise of intelligence and curiosity that is implicit in the experimental behaviors of their teenagers, and to give their encouragement supportively and unobtrusively, as they did when their little ones were learning to crawl and walk. They have the power to exercise the "first principle" of family relationships described in Chapter 1. And they have the power to understand and accept that their offspring's rejection of the parent is about the offspring, not about the parent.

If I reject you, that is a statement of my values, and my perception. It does not change you, or make you less valuable or worthwhile. If my teenager says to me, "You are a bad father," that does not make me a bad father. It is a statement by my teenager about what he values in a father figure. I'm interested in that. I'm interested in how he forms his judgments and about how he applies them to himself. I can "make him right" by valuing his groping toward a set of values and standards about fatherhood and fathering. I can encourage his pursuit of information and knowledge on that subject. I can support his effort to make himself a better father than I was, if only by his standards. And I can respect his development of wisdom on the subject of his choice.

But all too many parents fall into the trap of trying, and failing, to convince their youngsters that the youngsters are on the wrong track, that they're using bad judgment, that they're consorting with bad friends, that they're lying, that their priorities need reordering. And all too many teenagers argue and defy and wear an almost perpetual anger.

What can be done? Here the concept of basing resolution on the relationship rather than on the content does not serve us as well as it has with other kinds of conflict, because many teenagers are not very convinced that the relationship is important. Indeed, their questioning of the value of the relationship is often the stated content of the conflict. Another difficulty is the parents' persistence in making the teenager wrong. There are, however, two seeds of hope. One is that the typical teenager (if there is such a person) seeks validation for himself or herself as a person. In my experience, teenagers are ready to turn to their parents if they can trust their parents to give them the validation they seek. The other seed of hope is that parents, for the most part, do seem to value the relationship, and are motivated to strengthen it.

I want to address parents' motivation first.

What Parents Can Do

1. Know What is Possible. In approaching your teenagers, first take a clear look at what is possible. The time is rapidly approaching, or has already arrived, when you can't *make* the kids do anything. In all likelihood this has been true for a long time, but the kids didn't know it. They thought you could make them do things; so they did those things. Now your teenagers are testing the reality of that assumption, and are finding, to their delight and fear, that you can't make them do anything. Therefore what they do at your demand is done voluntarily. It may be done to avoid consequences that you impose, but the decision to avoid those consequences by delivering the required behavior is theirs. Physical coercion at this age is not at all as effective as it once was—if it ever was—and carries with it the danger of retaliatory brutality. So our choices seem to be (a) persuasion, (b), the threat of coercive consequences, and (c) finding some way to achieve consensus and mutual commitment.

Persuasion seldom works. Besides being a Communication Stopper (see Chapter 5), it is often an argument provoker.

Coercion carries with it the disadvantage that, although it may produce the desired behavior, it defines the relationship as one based on coercive power. Its net effect on the relationship is alienating.

2. Seek Consensus. Persuasion and coercion having been ruled out, this leaves consensus. How can you get consensus? By making sure that you and the other person emerge feeling like winners. How can you make your teenager a winner when, for example, he does not come home at the time he promised, he chooses friends whom you suspect of antisocial acts, he smokes pot, he denies that he smokes pot, he cuts classes in school, etc., etc.?

Various families try various approaches. Some of them succeed; others don't. Use what wisdom and experience you have acquired in your life. Maybe it will help to know that some leaders in this field have "struck out," some more than just once or twice. Consider the following suggestions.

    a. Remember to express your love. This is often forgotten in the heat of combat.

    b. When you get a loving stroke, acknowledge it if you want to encourage more.

    c. Be real. If you have been stuck in trying to appear to be what you're not, announce that you're giving it up.

    d. Announce your acceptance of your teenagers just as they are. They don't have to be anything else. But they can choose to be a different way if they so choose.

    e. Acknowledge that your teenager wants to be a separate person, unique. Don't be surprised if this separate person adopts values and beliefs different from yours.

    f. Make it clear that you want the same leeway.

    g. Review your time schedules from time to time; make sure you are making priority time available to the members of your family.

   h. Listen. Then feed back in your own words what you think you heard. Do this without negative judgments.

   i. Avoid such words as lie, cheat, steal.

   j. Don't give advice. You may offer your own experiences, but don't expect them to be accepted.

   k. Acknowledge that your teenager's body belongs to him or her. Don't nag him or her about nourishment, smoking, overeating, late hours.

   l. Remember: if you make them wrong, you will lose.

What Teenagers Can Do

1. Active listen. As I see it, the biggest thing that teenagers can do to make themselves winners in conflicts with their parents is to read and apply the chapters in this book that discuss active listening. In my experience, when a parent gets the message from a teenager that he or she has been heard and the message received, much of the parent's hostility and frustration and resistance vanish.

2. Give up blaming. Blaming puts the power "out there." Also, it makes your parents "wrong." Every time you make your parents wrong, you stiffen their resistance. Instead, can you make them right without making yourself wrong?

If they won't let you use the car as much as you would like, blaming would be, "You never let me use the car as much as I want to. I drive better than most of the other kids. You don't trust me." That approach is likely to be perceived as an attack, and is likely to produce defensiveness and resistance in your parents. A different approach might be, "When you don't let me use the car, I feel untrusted and discounted. I wish you would present your expectations so that I could have something to live up to, instead of giving me your doubts and suspicions so that I feel put down. I know you have physical safety at heart, but the method you are using feels to me like it is damaging the relationship."

If you get "grounded" for failing to come home at a promised time, you might try giving up blaming and arguing in favor of "making them right" in a way that does not make you wrong.

16

Dissolution of Marriage

DISSOLUTION OF MARRIAGE does not always represent a failure. Some-times it does, as when it comes about because one or both of the marital partners have failed to apply principles of good communication, or have shown inadequate care or concern for the other party, or have distorted the relationship by diplacing onto it attitudes and perceptions and patterns from past relationships. Some dissolutions, however, repre-sent a recognition by one or both of the parties that their values, goals, or interests are so divergent and incompatible that their growth—and sometimes their health—would be better served by their living apart. In these situations, the function of a marriage and family counselor may be to facilitate not the repair and rehabilitation of a marriage, but its constructive dissolution.

Fear of Alternatives

Sometimes the chief or only element holding a marriage together is that one or both of the partners are afraid of the alternatives. Some marital partners express this as a fear of the unknown. It may have been a long time since the partner was single, and the single life seems strange and unfamiliar and scary. Sometimes a partner fears that he or she will never be sought or accepted by another person, and that a lifetime of loneliness lies ahead. Sometimes people, particularly women, fear being exploited by new persons who seem attractive and make loving promises, but then take advantage of one, betray the trust given, and turn away, leaving tears in their wake. Women who have lost or never acquired marketable skills often fear material or financial insecurity. Mothers of young children often fear parenting their children without the aid of a husband and father in the home.

These examples by no means cover the full gamut of the fears I have heard expressed about taking steps to dissolve a marital relationship, but they are a fair sampling.

Some of these fears prove, with experience, to have been overdrawn. Others are quite well-founded. Some men and women express the fear, for instance, that nobody "out there" will like them or find them attractive. And women who have been homemakers may feel totally ignorant of how to apply for a job, much less support themselves. With time and experience, many of them discover their own assets and reduce their fears. But I have heard both men and women say that if they had realized how lonely they would be and how long they would be alone, they might not have severed their marital ties.

These fears put their victims in a double bind. On the one hand, the marriage is seen as intolerable. On the other hand, the anticipated consequences of dissolution are seen as so scary that the victim is tempted to continue in the intolerable relationship.

At this point, the victim of the fear has a difficult choice to make. One option is to remain in the relationship in order not to suffer the fear or the feared consequences. The other option is to work on the fear, to risk the consequences, and to take steps to terminate the marital relationship.

When the chosen option is to remain in the relationship, ways must be found to counteract feelings of helplessness, defeat, and despair. These feelings can quickly turn to repressed anger and depression. One antidote is to lay out and to pursue a pattern of growth and self-realization that will keep the person in touch with her or his power of choice and competence, and supply caring strokes from persons important in his or her life.

Children

Sometimes marital partners who would otherwise prefer to dissolve their relationship express a feeling that they should remain together "for the sake of the children." This is usually a way of expressing a conviction that children are better off with two parents in the home than with only one; so these couples use the often-heard phrase, "broken homes."

Having heard the cries and seen the tears of adults who grew up in homes with only one parent, and in loveless homes with two parents, I see that the big question is not whether the parents remain together. The welfare of children is best served by parents who feel good about themselves and who express genuine love for their children. Without these ingredients, the children are going to suffer whether the parents stay together or not.

Some negative consequences of staying together "for the sake of the children" are the following. The children witness few if any expressions of love between the parents, and may grow up ignorant of or blind to the kinds of loving gestures that flow naturally and spontaneously between loving partners. If there is continuing conflict, the children may develop a host of negative attitudes and feelings toward conflict, argument, or even marriage itself. The children may sense that the parents continue to endure their ordeal "because of the children," and may come to feel a sense of responsibility or even guilt for the ordeal through which they see their parents going.

Some of the negative consequences of living in a single-parent home are the following. The children may be deprived of exposure to acts of loving communication that flow naturally and spontaneously between partners in a loving relationship. Visitation times with the absent parent may take on a holiday or entertainment quality that renders unreal the relationship with and perception of the visiting parent. If the custodial parent is bitter toward the absent parent, the children's perceptions of the absent parent may become distorted, and perceptions of all members of the absent parent's sex may similarly be distorted.

These distortions need not occur. Parents who take and maintain steps to acquire and sustain high self-esteem can provide their children with adequate love and realistic perceptions, whether or not they remain together for "the sake of the children."

Settlement Agreement

Usually arrangements must be made for division of property, payment of debts, child support, alimony (by whatever name it may be called), custody and education of children, and visitation. A thoughtful, provident, realistic agreement on these matters can go far toward reducing whatever bitterness may be present and toward eliminating, or at least reducing, future friction.

Sometimes, when the marital partners can't agree, the settlement is made by court order. Seldom is a court order as equitable and satisfactory as what the parties themselves might have worked out, with their more intimate knowledge of the facts.

One common error made by parties to a settlement agreement on dissolution of marriage is overgenerosity. Sometimes a party feels so eager or relieved to get out of a conflict-ridden marriage that she or he gives up far more than sober reflection would dictate. At the other extreme, sometimes one party or the other is able to exert such pressure that the advantages gained will be a constant source of resentment and friction.

With many couples, the effects of a settlement agreement must be lived with for a long time. These effects can perpetuate or exacerbate hurts and frictions, or they can provide a solid take-off place from which both sides can go on to new, relatively friction-free existences.

Lawyers

In my judgment, providing adequate legal representation for husbands and wives in divorce proceedings is a legal specialty that requires training and continuing experience. Not all specialists in this field provide equally satisfactory service. Some clients seek a divorce lawyer who is known to be aggressive and sometimes even merciless. In my experience, the lawyers who meet this description may be equally aggressive and merciless with their own clients, and may stand in the way of an equitable settlement. They may even bring about harsh judgments and ongoing conflicts.

A common complaint against lawyers is that they do not answer their telephone calls. Another is that they do not listen well to their clients and that, as a result, the clients do not feel well-represented.

One way to find a satisfactory attorney is to inquire among friends whose judgment you trust and who have gone through divorce proceedings with the help of an attorney. Another way is to consult lawyers of your acquaintance whose judgment you trust. A third way is to call the local bar association or lawyer referral service, and describe the kind of lawyer you want. It is prudent, in calling the lawyer of your choice, to describe to him or her what kind of attorney you are looking for, and to judge then whether the attorney's description of himself or herself meets your needs and sounds convincing. It is also prudent to arrange for an introductory interview in order to get an impression of the lawyer before committing the case to his or her care.

Some couples prefer "do-it-yourself" divorces, because lawyers add to the cost of the dissolution. Often enough both parties prefer to be represented by the same lawyer, so that they don't have to pay two legal fees. Good legal service requires reasonable legal fees, and, like medical fees or repair bills, these are unwelcome costs, but they can be minimized. One way is to discuss fees at the outset of the interview with your attorney, and to make your situation clear. Many attorneys are willing to adjust their fees in case of need. And there is wide variation in the fees that attorneys charge.

In 27 years of law practice, I found few instances in which it was totally satisfactory for both parties to be represented by one lawyer. The retention of two attorneys may double the legal fees, but usually the added protection is worth the difference.

Marriage Counselors

There is a growing body of literature and practice on the subject of marriage, family, and child counseling. In some places, such as California, the field has been so professionalized that a state license is required. In other places, anybody may hang out a sign. Some persons who do hang out signs in these places are admirable, skilled, and competent. Others are not. Even among persons who are skilled, qualified, and licensed in marriage and family counseling, divorce counseling is not a subject in which all are thoroughly experienced.

Even among the experienced counselors, a few operate with biases or prejudices that they do not reveal and of which they are sometimes not even aware. One such bias, for example, may be that the marriage should be preserved at almost any cost. Another is that married women should take certain roles, married men other roles.

Competence as a psychotherapist does not necessarily confer competence as a marriage or family therapist. One skill that a good marriage and family counselor has is the ability to observe, evaluate, and comment on family process, dynamics, and systems. Even among the best psychiatrists and psychologists, not all have developed skills in these areas of interaction. At the same time, competence in family process does not in itself confer clinical excellence in individual growth and development. A good choice is a counselor who brings together the special learnings and skills required for both individual and interpersonal counseling.

Here are a few sources at which to inquire in trying to obtain adequate divorce (or marriage) counseling:

the local office of the American Association of Marriage and Family Counselors;
the local office of the California Association of Marriage and Family Therapists;
the referee or judge of the local conciliation court, if there is one;
the judge or referee of the local domestic relations court;
members of the clergy, particularly those who are willing to give

candid evaluations of the skills and performances of local pastoral counselors;

humanist counselors;

attorneys who have wide experience with divorce cases.

friends who have been able to find satisfactory divorse counsel.

PART FIVE

The Ever-Renewing Relationship

17

The Ever-Renewing Relationship

Is it possible?

Is it really possible to recapture in your loving relationship the excitement, the newness, the freshness of that urgent, tremulous, hope-filled reaching for and discovering each other that characterized your relationship at its formation?

I think it is. My mother and father were in their middle eighties when they died, but up to the very end I saw them holding hands wherever they were. My Mom would utter some witty remark, and I would see my Dad's eyes sparkle with appreciation. Then he would turn to us and say, "I'll leave it to you. Isn't she a cutie!" At 85, she was a "cutie" to him. Partially blind, her back bent, her chest collapsed, her fingers gnarled, and her skin creased by a thousand lines, she was a cutie. And so she thrived in the sunshine of his appreciation. I cannot count the number of times my mother told me—each time as though it were new information—that since meeting my Dad, she had never met another man with whom she could be content.

What was their secret? When their hands sought the other's hands as they watched television, or as they sat with family or friends, what was the quality in their gesture that made it plain, to me at least, that this was a gesture with fresh meaning in their awareness each time they did it?

Realistic Recommitment

I know that I change over time. I see this in others too. I wake up today. I have today's experiences. I am influenced and shaped by those experiences. I incorporate them into myself, so that I can adapt intelligently to my environment and cope with it competently. My self-esteem rises or falls as I experience my competence, integrity, belonging, uniqueness, and sense-making power. Whether greatly or minutely, I am transformed from day to day, moment to moment.

And the same is true of my partner. The very act of choosing me to be her partner is a transforming experience, makes her a different person. The person who chose me is no more. The person I chose is no more. By the act of choosing, we have made ourselves different from the persons we were when we chose each other.

Now I have a momentous choice. I can close myself off from this stranger until I have evidence that the new relationship is safe. Or I can begin the process of discovering who this stranger is and revealing to her who I am.

Either of those choices initiates a never-ending process. If I close myself off because my partner is a stranger, my closing off is a transforming experience to my partner. And, being transformed, my partner is again a stranger. And again, and again. If, instead, I explore who my partner is and reveal who I am, that, too, is a transforming experience to my partner. And, being transformed, my partner is again a stranger. And again, and again.

So the commitment I have received from my partner is a commitment by the person she was when she made it, to the person I was when she made it. Does she (whoever she now is) still make it to me (whoever I have become)? Actually, all she can realistically give me is her present intention. What commitment will be made by the person she will be tomorrow or next year is conjecture.

In our classes on the ever-renewing relatioship, Marion and I begin to hear at this point: "But you're saying that promises aren't worth anything!"

"If this were true, what would happen to marriage vows?"

"Then how can agreements be enforced?"

I want to make it clear that I take agreements very seriously. I also take reality very seriously. One of our realities is that the traditional marriage vow is made "until death do us part" or in similar words that imply foreverness. Another is that nearly half of all marriages terminate in divorce or dissolution. Clearly, some relationships intended to last forever or at least for the lives of the parties fall considerably short of either mark.

Even though divorce is now common, and many causes of divorce are clearly and commonly recognized, most persons contracting marriage appear to believe that divorce will not happen to them. Likewise, many persons facing the termination of a relationship experience a sense of failure and a feeling of guilt that the marriage did not endure as long as they had promised or intended that it would.

I'd like to see marital vows brought more into line with what are currently realistic expectations. If I promise or choose what I know I can do, I'm a winner; if I promise or choose what I can't do, I'm a loser. Clearly, if I contract a marriage today to last "until death do us part," my chances of being a winner are only a little better than 50-50, maybe less.

Yet most couples with whom I've dealt want to make some commitment more binding and more lasting than a mere declaration of joining only for this moment. For these couples, let me offer a declaration born of my own experience. It is, in fact, the declaration that I have made to my partner and is the essence of my daily commitment.

"I haven't words sufficient to expresss to you the depth and completeness of my commitment to you as your partner in this relationship. My present intention is that this commitment will be for as long as I can foresee. What I know from my own experience, and from my experience of others, is that I can't foretell, let alone promise, what my intent will be in the future. I can't even tell what kind of person I will be, or what kind of person you will be, since we are both in the process of continuing to change. So the commitment I make now without reservation is only for now, which is all I have.

"Since the only commitment I can make is a commitment for now, a part of my present intention is to look at you anew and afresh each day—each moment—and to look at myself in the same way. I want to court you again, and invite you again, and commit to you again, and seek your commitment again, with all the freshness and stimulation and delight and excitement of a new relationship.

"This means giving up a lot of 'comfortable' patterns that I see other couples 'enjoying.' I can't assume that you'll do the cooking and that I'll make the beds as we did yesterday; new relationship means new contract. I can't assume the continuing renewal of your commitment to me. This gives me great anxiety, but also inspires me to pay keen, continuing attention to your wants, preferences, and values. That kind of alertness and readiness to reevluate and adjust takes take a lot of my focus, energy, attention, and time.

"And here's the hardest part. The process of continuous review and reevaluation implies that there may come a day when you choose *not* to recommit to me—or I to you. However, this process helps us to catch and correct little flaws before they escalate into big ones. Even so, sometimes I yearn for a more peaceful way. So far it has eluded me.

"So I commit to you for *this* moment, perhaps even for this day, and I invite you to commit to me for this moment, perhaps even for this day. I know you can't speak for the person you'll be tomorrow. So that will be a day of courtship to discover each other with all the joy and solemnity of another first time."

Listening, Holding, Being There

While we are anxiously waiting to see who we will be tomorrow, isn't there something we can do? The good news is, yes, there are some wondrous things we can do.

Listening

One is to listen. Oh, how I wish I could impart passion to the written word when I urge you *to listen*. The floors of my office are drenched with the tears of wives and husbands, sons and daughters, fathers and mothers, brothers and sisters who have been thirsting just to be *heard* by those important to them in their lives. Oh, yes, they get a hearing of sorts, but what they get back are words of argument or advice or reassurance or "Tut, tut" or "Me too" or the other Communication Stoppers listed in Chapter 5. Or worse, they get "I'm too busy," or "That's your problem," or "You're taking it much too seriously," or "Don't cry."

For the ever-renewing relationship, whether it be lover to lover, parent to child, or whatever, *be there* for your partner. Just be there and listen, acceptantly. You don't have to agree; just listen. You don't have to understand; just listen.

Not just to the words (although words are important); tune in on the whole person: the feelings under the words, the perception of the world as it looks and feels to that person about whom you care.

And when you have listened, find out whether you have heard. Your partner says, "Oh, God, I'm so lonely," and you say, "Feeling all alone in the world," and suddenly your partner is no longer alone in the world. You have joined him or her there by listening and by reflecting back what you have heard. And in so doing you have validated your partner, shored up her or his self-esteem, at least partially filled his or her cup, and enriched the relationship between you.

Does it sound like active listening? It is active listening. But it is more than the mechanics of Chapters 4 through 6. It is an investment in the other's life. It is the cosmic assertion, "You are not alone. I am here with you. I am testifying that You Are."

If I can do that empathically, I can testify not only that You Are, but also that the way you are is just fine. When I hear that from you, I love you. I don't know why I love you just because you heard me empathically and have fed back acceptantly what you have heard. I don't even know what love is. But I know it when I experience it. And I experience it when my loved one affirms my place in the world, my OK-ness in it just as I am, my right to be where I am *as I am*, and to be heard and included without conditions or qualifications or judgments.

The more I see of love—when it is present and when it is lacking—the more it seems to me to be a surge of joining, thankfulness, trust, relief, and joy at the experience of being validated, okayed. So if I want to renew my relationships—and renew them again and again—one way I know for doing that is to listen, and, having listened, to hear, and, having heard, to reflect back to my partner that I have heard empathically, acceptantly, affirmingly.

Holding

Sometimes all that is required is to hold your partner. More times than I can count, I have heard women sob, "I would like, sometimes when I reach out, just to be held and not to be used sexually," or "It took me a long time to realize that I have been trading sex for the holding that I really want." With many men, their yearning to be held has been buried so deeply they are no longer aware of it. Offers by their partners to hold them may be experienced as awkward or embarrassing. To the partners of these men, I would recommend that you offer your holding if the offer is genuine for you, but that you not push it, and certainly that you not "mind read" your partner's desire for holding if he himself is not in touch with it.

Being There

Sometimes all that is required for the ever-renewing relationship is just to be there—not active listening, not holding, but just being there.

At the same time, I am aware that just being there is seldom enough. Couples and families in counseling talk a lot about spending time, giving time, being there. But it isn't just time and presence that is renewing. The healing, enriching, renewing quality of being there depends on the intent that it expresses. To be with you and to be dead is not renewing. To be with you reluctantly, resentfully, distractedly is not renewing. To be there for you is renewing when the message you get from my being there is that I *want* to be there, with *you*, because I value you, and that I express that value by making an affirmative choice to be with you from among all my choices. And, having chosen to be with you, I give quality to our time together and to my presence with you by giving you my focus, my attention, in ways which give you messages that you can translate into self-esteem. Out of this elevation of self-esteem love grows.

Empathy

To nurture the ever-renewing relationship by listening, holding, being there, implies the capacity for empathy. We have looked at empathy before (in Chapter 6), and made note of its healing quality. Can you give empathy? If you don't do it as well as you want, can you do better? I think you can. And if your partner seems to be giving less empathy than you would like, can he or she do better? That depends on whether your partner wants to make that change for you.

Sometimes my capacity to give empathy is limited or blocked by distractions in my life. These distractions may be distractions of the moment: I have a headache or an urgent need to go to the bathroom; I am late for work; somebody sits on my hat. Or these distractions may be products of my history: when you express anxiety about money, I remember how my friend next door used money to exploit me, and I react defensively to that memory instead of being where you are. Or these distractions may grow out of my history with you: when you express a desire for sexual play with me, I remember angrily the times that you have rejected my sexual advances.

Distractions of the moment need not impair empathy, particularly if they are verbalized and faced together. Distractions that grow out of our history together can be dissipated by resolving those old conflicts constructively. Family, marriage, and couple counseling by therapists well-trained in systems and process concepts can be helpful in working out these unfinished issues.

Distractions and blocks that are rooted in experiences from my formative years may be harder to remove, and may require psychotherapy of one kind or another. (I am grateful for my own therapy and for the dissipation of distortions, distractions, and blocks that I worked out in those sessions, sometimes with great pain.)

Without those distractions, I am better able to open myself to the important others in my life, to give them my attention, my focus, my caring, with a minimum of critical judgment. And when I do that, I see the other persons' self-esteem elevated, their bodies relax, and their love for me renewed.

In Chapter 6, I looked briefly at intuition. Empathy is an intuitive process. When I open myself to *feel* what it is like to be the other person, I can feel—not just understand, although understanding is included— how that person's behavior, his or her stance in life, flows logically, sometimes almost inexorably, from that person's life experience up to this moment. Often, when I do that, I get a surprise: suddenly it all comes clear to me why that person is as he or she is. As I draw on my intuition, I become suddenly aware *within myself* of feelings, attitudes, and perceptions in that other person of which I had never before been aware. Where I had seen stubbornness, I become aware of feelings of insecurity underlying the stubbornness. Where I had seen defensiveness, I become aware of that person's fear. From that I begin to intuit the pain in my partner, and I can care about the pain.

Almost every empathic message is an exercise in intuition, in getting the feel of what it is like to be the other person, in picking up minimum clues from that person's words, voice, body, and context, and in processing those clues in such a way that the other person's way of being makes sense and order in the framework of that person's experience.

At our Center, I often hear people say, "I can't do all that." What I see is that they can do it: haltingly at first for some of them; then with increasing facility and effectiveness as they allow themselves to experiment, and to act as if they were doing it; and then increasingly to do it.

That is the way we learned to walk. We didn't wait to have it explained to us and then to "understand" it. We walked. We gave ourselves the experience of walking. We learned to do it by doing it. Awkwardly at first, with lots of falling down and skinned knees and falls from places imprudently risked. But we did it. And, similarly, we can acquire skill in intuition, empathy, and awareness of feelings by doing it.

Reducing Isolation

One way to enliven a relationship is to get out among other people. It has been my observation that many couples who complain of dead relationships or of depression have few good friends either separately or as a couple.

I am not urging an active or busy social life unless that is already something that you like. I am suggesting that if one partner can have at least one supportive person in whom he or she can confide and for whom he or she can be a supportive friend, and if the couple together can share in that manner with a friend or another couple, then knowing those three or four people could make an important difference.

How are such friendships formed? Usually, I would say, they occur in the course of doing what you like to do.

Rita liked to take long walks in the out-of-doors. Usually these were solitary events. On my suggestion she joined the Sierra Club and found others who shared many of her interests.

Tom liked working with his hands. He also needed furniture for his bachelor apartment when he became single again. He combined these two issues, and took a wood-shop class in night school. He struck up a friendship with the teacher and a fellow student.

Jackie took a brown-bag lunch with her on a new job, and found herself ignored by the other workers. So she asked these old-timers whether she could join them and found herself welcomed.

Courtship and Merriment

Can you remember back to the days (and far into the nights) when you and your partner-to-be were engaged in those first, golden, exciting explorations of each other? The focus you gave and got? The sensitivity to the other's needs, wants, preferences, and desires? The little (and big) gestures and services given to please the other? The putting of your best foot forward?

What became of those searching looks you bent to the discovery of your partner's uniqueness? The time you set aside to give full attention to each other? An "I love you" card sent for no special occasion? A poem you wrote?

These gestures can work their magic even in relationships of long standing. And in long-term relationships that function well, I see the partners engaged over and over again in the little rituals and observances that we think of as typical of courtship.

Marion makes a lunch for me to take to work, a gesture that I interpret as caring. And she places a little heart or love note on the outside. Yes, every day. And because I value those acts of caring, I try to make sure to voice my pleasure.

Probably the most basic courtship gesture is concerned focus, the kind of attention that accompanies the effort fully to hear and understand the other's meaning, feelings, and intentions.

Along with that are the gestures that say, "I like to be with you." I reach for your hand. I move to be closer to where you are doing something.

I also appreciate you and what you do. When we are with others, I include you in what I say. I am attentive to what you say, and I am appreciative of what you say and do even when we disagree. I appreciate your tastes and values even when they are not mine.

I pay special attention to the pride and pleasure you take in creating something or doing a task well, even if it is no more grand than cleaning a room or making a hamburger. I am alert to changes you have made in yourself or in your surroundings.

I take delight in giving you pleasure, whether by gifts or by compliments or by appreciative attention and notice.*

One couple with whom I worked agreed on a signal to help each other give appreciative attention. When Meg got a new hairdo or made some other change that she wanted Matt to notice, she wore a gold pendant that Matt had given her. When Matt wanted Meg's notice, he wore his gold-plated identification tag. On one occasion, when Meg wanted Matt to notice a new perfume of hers, she wore her pendant as a signal. Matt guessed new hairdo. No. New nightgown. No. New face powder. No. The guessing game produced frustration, but also giggles. As a final hint, Meg steamed the label off her perfume bottle and pasted it behind her ear. That did it, and cracked them up with laughter.

That raises the subject of merriment. At a workshop I attended on the scientific study of sex, a report was made on sexual patterns among elderly people. One of the findings was that merriment is important in forming and maintaining gratifying relationships. The report was limited to the sexual aspect of relationships with persons over 65 years of age but, sensitized by that report, I have observed that merriment is an important—perhaps indispensable—element in just about all ongoing relationships, sexual and otherwise. So have a good time.

Love,
Mendel and Marion

---

*Of several sources of experiments and exercises for freshening perceptions of each other, I recommend *Me, You, and Us*, by Dr. Gerald Walker Smith and Alice I. Phillips, and *Growth Games* by Howard R. Lewis and Dr. Harold S. Straitfeld.

Appendix A. The Language of Parent, Adult, Child

Here and there in this book, I have found it convenient and clarifying to use some of the language I learned from Transactional Analysis (sometimes referred to as TA). Rather than digressing to define those terms in the text, I would like to define them here, not necessarily as they are used by practitioners of TA but simply as I use them in this book.

1. *Parent, Adult, Child*

I have used the terms Parent, Adult, and Child (P, A, and C) as the names of three "ego states" that every person may be said to have (Figure A.1). A person is born in a Child ego state. The Parent and Adult ego states are developed by experience and the process of growing up and maturing. The Parent and Adult as they develop do not supplant the Child ego state; they supplement it. In the fully developed person, all three ego states are available to the individual, often in rapid sequence.

For example, I trip over my daughter's bicycle on my front porch. I am startled and afraid. Those feelings and emotions are in my Child. I

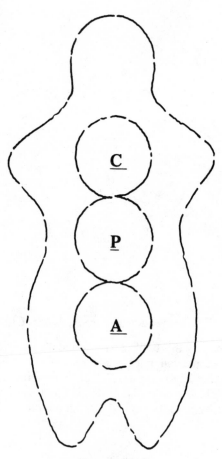

FIGURE A.1.

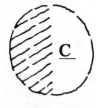

FIGURE A.2.

FIGURE A.3.

FIGURE A.4.

realize the bike has been left where it should not have been left, and I condemn this violation of the rules. That critical judgment is in my Parent. I make a quick calculation about the best way to prevent repetitions of this accident. In doing so I am in my Adult.

Child. I find it convenient to think of the Child ego state as having two parts. One part is the Natural Child, the other the Adapted Child (Figure A.2). The Natural Child has all the feelings, emotions, senses, and impulses with which we are naturally invested, and expresses itself in laughter, tears, joy, sorrow, and impulsive, spontaneous behavior.

The Adapted Child is the child that has learned ways of responding to the rules, commands, and limitations of the human and physical environment. The Adapted Child typically expresses itself by protesting, rebelling, manipulating, placating, accommodating, and avoiding. We can each identify some or all of these behaviors in ourselves, no matter how old we grow, and no matter how strong an Adult we may have developed.

Parent. The Parent ego state may also be considered to be in two parts: the Nurturing Parent and the Critical Parent (Figure A.3). The Nurturing Parent expresses itself in nurturing, accepting, and supportive attitudes and behaviors. The process of active listening explained in Chapters 4 to 6 is an example of behavior coming from the Nurturing Parent.

The Critical Parent is the repository of rules, shoulds, musts, requirements, moral judgments, social requirements and the so-called wisdom of the race. Your Critical Parent is a storehouse of items resulting from countless choices on your part to store those items and to make them "true" or "right." Your Critical Parent, as a result, can keep you out of trouble by keeping you convinced that it is wrong to steal. It can also get you into trouble by keeping you in the grip of prejudices, such as that all men are untrustworthy or all women are out to get your money.

Adult. The Adult ego state may be likened to a computer. It takes in information, processes it, decides its significance to the individual, and makes choices based on the information so received and processed. Some of the information received by the Adult comes from the Child and Parent ego states. The Adult monitors the other ego states, because they contain and represent information vital to the individual. That I feel rage in my Child ego state is important information to me. That my Parent ego state may condemn destructive behavior is also important information. In my Adult I process both of these items of information, along with data received from outside, such as the laws pertaining to murder and the findings of psychologists on the consequences of repressing rage. Combining this information I am able, in my Adult ego state, to make decisions and choices that serve my best short-term and long-range interests.

2. OK-ness

In TA terms the most desirable life position a person can take is "I'm OK, you're OK." Most of us, in growing up, seem to take the position "I'm not OK, you're OK," because we see ourselves as small and feeble and lacking in many of the skills and powers that our parents and teachers have. Effective parenting is the process of reinforcing the child's sense of OK-ness, and at the same time, by precept and example, establishing the parents' own OK-ness in the child's eyes.

For the most part, I have used the terms OK and OK-ness to signify basic worthwhileness, not conditioned on doing "well" or being "good," but predicated simply on the individual's innate right to be. "I'm OK" is therefore an assertion of one's is-ness, much as the law of gravity might say self-acceptantly, "I'm OK." And if the law of gravity then tipped its hat to the Earth's 24-hour rotation around its axis, it could add, "You're OK." Each assertion is, at one level, an assertion simply of what is. At another level it is an affirmation that the way it is works, that it could not rightly be another way, that if it were another way, it would not be what it is. In that sense, "I'm OK, you're OK" means I'm all right just as I am, including the rightness of any choice I make to change or not, and you're all right (for you, even though you may not fit for me) just as you are, including the rightness of any choice you may make to change or not.

3. Strokes

In my terminology, strokes are acts of recognition (I am indebted to TA for the idea and the word). The assumption is that everybody needs strokes in order to survive. It has been observed that newborn infants need more than warmth, feeding, and dry clothing. If they do not also receive fondling, handling, touching, the sounds of voices talking to them, or other signs of emotional nurturance, their development is impaired, and some of them do not survive. Human beings (with exceptions such as schizophrenics and autistic children) exhibit the need for stroking in many ways. They seek to please those from whom they may get loving strokes. Many of the them have learned to ask for physical stroking. And rather than get no strokes at all, many have learned to get negative strokes, in the form of words or looks of disapproval, or of punishment.

4. *Scripts or Programs*

Another concept for which I am indebted to Transactional Analysis is the notion of scripts. As I use the term, it proceeds from the observation that every human being with enough intelligence to exercise choices begins at birth, and continues throughout life, to try to make sense and order out of his or her world of experience. Making sense and order is a process of deciding which experiences are significant and which are not, and how those experiences fit together. As a part of this process, the individual makes decisions about who he or she is, and about whether he or she is OK. Other decisions may include whether I am a winner or a loser, whether I am to be a joyful or joyless person, what kind of marriage I shall make, what occupation I shall follow, and many more. This pattern of decisions is called a script. Most scripts seem to be constructed in the period between birth and ages five to eight. After that the individual tends to filter out or distort new experience that does not conform with his or her script; so the script is constantly reinforced by new experiences that appear to confirm the early decisions, and is not disturbed by new experience that does not conform to those decisions. New decisions may be made, however, and new scripts may be written when an individual, during the course of psychotherapy or otherwise, decides to reparent himself or herself with permission to change and to be OK in the new mode.

Appendix B. Other Terms

1. *Old Tapes*

I think of an old tape as an attitude, perception, or reaction left over from another time and not necessarily appropriate to the present situation. For example, suppose Marion becomes angry with me, and I perceive her anger as dangerous to me. The danger signals come from an old memory tape in which, when I was very little, my father's loud, angry voice seemed to me to threaten my very survival.

2. *Hooked*

If you order me to do something, I am very likely to experience rebellious feelings. One way of expressing this phenomenon is to say that my rebellious Child gets hooked. My Child can get hooked in lots of ways. A friend says, "You're not listening to me." I respond indignantly, "I am too." I let my defensive Child get hooked.

My Parent can also get hooked. My daughter uses a four-letter word, and I punish her because her use of such language violates my moral code. My Parent is said to be hooked.

3. *Fight*

Here and there, and particularly in Chapter 8, I have used the word "fight" to refer to a transaction entered into to resolve a conflict. No need to be scared. The kind of "fight" to which I refer is not a destructive or hurting fight. It is an encounter entered into in order (a) to resolve the subject matter in dispute and (b), at the same time, to strengthen and enliven the relationship. If you are saying to yourself, "That isn't a fight," I would like to ask you to move over one step, and say, "All right, Mendel, that isn't what *fight* ordinarily means to me, but I hear how you are using it."

Appendix C. Terminology for Feelings

1. *Feelings Connected with Senses*

Here are some words for feelings connected with the senses:

Eyes	Temperature	Pressure	Pain
dazzled	cold/hot	crushed	agony
	cool/warm	hemmed in	anguish
	flushed	light/heavy	hurt
		pressure	pain
		pushed	sore
		relief	suffer

Taste/ alimentary	Breathing	Total body	
disgust	breathless	alert	nervous
full/empty	choked up	alive/dead	refreshed
hunger	drowning	apathy	relaxed
like/dislike	smothered	comfort	restless
nausea	strangled	dispirited	sick/well
revulsion	suffocated	distress	small/big
sated/satisfied		drained	soft/hard
starved		empty/full	tense/tension/
thirst		energetic	relaxed
		excited	tired
		exhausted	weak/strong
		jittery	
		misery	

2. *Feelings Accompanying Bodily Reactions*

I would also go beyond the direct experience of the sense receptors, and would include the many kinds of feelings that accompany tears, laughter, flushing, trembling, sweating, and sometimes diarrhea and vomiting.

Some of the feelings that accompany tears are:

frustration	relief
grief	sadness
joy	sorrow
loneliness	tenderness

as well as the warm, tender components of tears, such as those experienced on being reunited with a loved one, or on being moved to tears by an honor accorded someone dear to us, or by a delightful performance by children.

I would include the many accompaniments of laughter, such as joy, delight, nervousness, anxiety, surprise, and the experiencing of humor.

Flushing and the sensation of heat that often accompanies flushing may indicate:

anger	sexual arousal
anxiety	threat
dread	

Diarrhea or vomiting may accompany feelings of terror, anxiety, helplessness.

3. *Primitive and Survival Sensations*

I would also include some of the survival sensations about which our bodies give us signals. Some of these signals are:

agitated	crazy	hate
alarmed	dazed	helplessness
angry	defeated	homesick
annoyed	defenseless	indignant
anxious	defensive	joy
apathetic	dismayed	lifeless/lively
apprehensive	enjoyment	like/dislike
astonished/ surprised	fear/afraid	moved/touched
bad/good	fury	pleased/displeased
bored/interested	glad	rage
calm	gloom	resentful
cheerful	grief	safe/unsafe
	happy/sad	shy

shocked	terror	upset
sorry	threat	worried
stunned	thrilled	
sure/secure/insecure	trapped	

4. *Feelings Related to Sexual and Love Needs*

Since the need for love strokes and belonging has many physical components, I would include feelings related to that need, such as:

ardent	friendly	lust
aroused	horny	passion
ashamed	jealous	rejected
affection	lonely	sexy
cut-off	loved/	turned on/off
ecstasy	unloved	uncared for

Loneliness may be either the kind that is felt in the desire to be with some significant person, or the kind that is the lot of each of us on recognizing our basic aloneness in, and responsibility for, our universe, no matter how well-favored we may be in the esteem and attention of those we love.

5. *Other Social Feelings*

attached	deprived	jealous
bitchy	devoted	rejected
caring	embarrassed	shame/ashamed
close	envious	sympathetic
compassionate	fond	tender
defiant	friendly	trusted, trusting
dependent/	guilty	unwanted
independent	humiliated	

6. *Sense of Self*

I want to include also as feelings those perceptions that give us our basic sense of self. Among these are the feelings (actually perceptions) that we can make sense and order out of our world; the feeling (perception) that we are competent in coping with our world; and the feeling (perception) that we are lovable, that we have a valued place in the family or tribal system of which we are a part, and that we matter, i.e., have the power to make a difference in it. (For a more complete discussion of these feelings or perceptions, see the discussion of self-esteem in Chapter 1.)

7. *Feelings Related to Place in the World*

acceptant	frustrated	regretful/remorseful/
calm	hopeless/hopeful	contrite
carefree	humble	secure/insecure
competent/	kind	split
incompetent	mischievous	torn
doubtful	patient/impatient	troublea
eager	proud	whole
enthused		

Appendix D. Using This Book as a Teaching Tool

Here are the course outlines that Marion and I use in teaching adult classes on "Resolving Family Conflicts so that Everybody Wins."

I. No-lose concept
    A. Making you right so that I can win; making me right so that you can win
    B. Winning in the relationship vs. winning on the issue; content vs. process
    C. Building self-esteem; reducing resistance and defensiveness
II. Basic communication skills
    A. Elements of communication process
       1. Sender's perception and awareness of self and others
       2. Communication diagram; multilevel messages (Figure A.5)
       3. Taking responsibility for being heard
    B. Active listening
       1. Utility
       2. Feelings, empathy, intuition, sensitivity, understanding
       3. Skill, practice, and innovation; role-play
    C. Communication Stoppers
    D. Clearing up hidden assumptions, fixed judgments, old perceptions
III. Conflict resolution
    A. No-lose practice; nurturing concept; effective parenting/teaching/managing/leading
       1. Counting self and other in
       2. Discipline and role perceptions
       3. Leveling, congruence

B. Skills
　　1. I-messages (with active listening)
　　2. Six-point problem solving
　　3. Fair-fight techniques; healing vs. alienating methods
C. Bridging age, sex, value and culture differences
D. Mediating conflicts among others

IV. Basic human relations
A. Transactional theory; OK-ness
B. Parenting and peoplemaking concepts
C. The ever-renewing relationship

When we come to that part of the course which deals with fair fighting, we use the following outlines.

I. Warm up (inner dialog)
A. What specific behaviors constitute the problem?
B. Who owns the problem?
C. Whose behavior is the problem?
D. How important is the relationship to me?
E. Can I fight fairly?
F. Do I want to call it fighting?

II. Encounter
A. Announce intention to fight; get agreement to fight now, or agree on time and place
B. Agree on ground rules (deutero-fights)
　　1. Receiver has right to (a) say yes, or (b) say no, or (c) get more information or time, or (d) make counterproposal
　　2. Recesses and returns
　　3. Equalizers of "psychological size"
　　4. Coercion or intimidation
C. Discuss prior stages

III. Fight
A. Define Problem
　　1. I-message: feelings, practical effects, "I want"
　　2. Defensive response
　　3. Active listen
B. Brainstorm
C. Evaluate and choose solution
D. Put into effect
E. Review and reevaluate

IV. Cool off
A. Inner dialog on fight style, effects, learnings
B. Make up
C. Identify unresolved issues

Atkin, Edith, and Estelle Rubin, *Part-Time Father.* New York:
Backn, George R., and H. Goldring. *Creative Aggression.* New York:
Avon, 1975.
Backn, George R., and Peter Wyden. *The Intimate Enemy: How to Fight
Fair in Love and Marriage.* New York: Wyden, 1969.
Berne, Eric. *Games People Play.* New York: Grove, 1964.
Boston Women's Health Book Collective. *Ourselves and Our Children:
A Book By and For Parents.* New York: Random House, 1978.
Boswell, Nelson. *TA for Busy People.* New York: Harper & Row, 1977.
Boyd, Fannie Lee, and Ruth Stovall. *A Handbook of Consumer Educa-
tion.* Boston: Allyn & Bacon, 1978.
Branden, Nathaniel. *Psychology of Romantic Love.* Los Angeles:
Tarcher, 1980.
Briggs, Dorothy Corkille. *Your Child's Self-Esteem.* Garden City:
Doubleday, 1970.
Broderick, Carlfred. *Couples: How to Confront Problems and Maintain
Loving Relationships.* New York: Simon & Schuster, 1979.
Bryson, Jeff, and Rebecca Bryson, eds. *Dual-Career Couples.* New
York: Human Sciences Press, 1978.
Callahan, Sidney Cornelia. *Parenting.* Baltimore: Penguin, 1973.
Campbell, Susan. *The Couples Journey.* San Luis Obispo: Impact Pub-
lishing, 1980.
Colgrove, Melba, Harold Bloomfield, and Peter McWilliams. *How to
Survive the Loss of a Love.* New York: Simon & Schuster—Lion
Press, 1976.
Davis, Ken, and Tom Taylor. *Kids and Cash: A Parent's Dilemma.* San
Diego: Oak Tree Publications, 1978.
De Spelder, Lynne A., and Nathalie Prettyman. *A Guidebook for Teach-
ing Family Living.* Boston: Allyn & Bacon, 1980.
Dyer, Wayne. *Pulling Your Own Strings.* New York: Crowell, 1978.
Your Erroneous Zones. New York: Funk and Wagnalls, 1976.
Eagan, Andrea Boroff. *Why Am I So Miserable If These Are The Best
Years of My Life?* Philadelphia: Lippincott, 1976.
Fast, Julius. *Body Language.* New York: Lippincott, 1970.
Fraiberg, Selma H. *The Magic Years.* New York: Scribner, 1959.

Freed, Alvin M. *TA for Kids*. Sacramento: Jalmar Press, 1970. *TA for Tots*. Sacramento: Jalmar Press, 1973. *TA for Teens and Other Important People*. Sacramento: Jalmar Press, 1976.

Friday, Nancy. *My Mother/My Self: A Daughter's Search for Identity*. New York: Delacorte, 1977.

Gardner, Richard A. *The Parent's Book About Divorce*. New York: Doubleday, 1977.

Gesell, Arnold, and Frances L. Ilg. *Infant and Child in the Culture of Today*. New York: Harper, 1943.

Ginot, Haime. *Between Parent and Teenager*. New York: MacMillan, 1969.

Goldberg, Herb. *The Hazards of Being Male*. New York: Nash, 1976. *The New Male, from Macho to Sensitive But Still All Male*. New York: Signet, 1979.

Gordon, Sol. *You*. New York: New York Times Book Company, 1975.

Gordon, Thomas. *Parent Effectiveness Training*. New York: Wyden, 1979.

Gould, Lois. *X: A Fabulous Child's Story*. New York: Daughters Publishing, 1978.

Gould, Roger L. *Transformations in Adult Life*. New York: Simon & Schuster, 1978.

Halpern, Howard. *Cutting Loose: An Adult Guide to Coming to Terms With Your Parents*. New York: Bantam, 1978.

Harris, Thomas. *I'm OK, You're OK*. New York: Harper & Row, 1967.

Howell, Mary. *Helping Ourselves: Families and the Human Network*. Boston: Beacon Press, 1977.

Hunt, Morton M. *World of the Formerly Married*. New York: McGraw, 1966.

Isaacs, Susan, and Marti Keller. *The Inner Parent: Raising Ourselves, Raising Our Children*. New York: Harcourt Brace Jovanovich, 1979.

James, Muriel, and Dorothy Jangeward. *Born to Win*. Menlo Park: Addison-Wesley, 1971.

Jourard, Sidney. *The Transparent Self*. New York: Van Nostrand, 1971.

Kassorla, Irene. *Putting It All Together*. New York: Warner Books, 1976.

Klemer, Richard H., and Rebecca McCulloch Smith. *Teaching About Family Relationships*. Minneapolis: Burgess, 1975.

Krantzler, Mel. *Creative Divorce*. New York: New American Library, 1975.

Levine, James A. *Who Will Raise Our Children? New Options for Fathers (and Mothers)*. Philadelphia: Lippincott, 1976.

Lewis, Howard R., and Harold S. Straitfeld. *Growth Games*. New York: Harcourt Brace, 1970.

Liswood, Rebecca. *First Aid for the Happy Marriage*. New York: Pocket Book, 1967.

McGinley, Phyllis. *Times Three*. New York: Viking, 1961.

Menninger, Karl. *The Crime of Punishment*. New York: Viking, 1968.

Miller, Sherod, Elam W. Nunnally, Daniel B. Wackman. *Alive and Aware: How to Improve Your Relationships Through Better Communication*. Minneapolis: Interpersonal Communication Programs, 1975.

Ms. Magazine, editors. *Free to Be . . . You and Me*. New York: Ms. Magazine Press, 1974.

Newman, Mildred, and Bernard Berkowitz. *How to Be Your Own Best Friend*. New York: Ballantine, 1974. *How to Take Charge of Your Life*. New York: Ballantine, 1978.

Noble, June, and William Noble. *How to Live With Other People's Children*. New York: Hawthorne, 1977.

Oaklander, Violet. *Windows to Our Children*. Moab, UT: Real People Press, 1978.

Ogden, Gina, and Anne Zevin. *When a Family Needs Therapy*. Boston: Beacon Press, 1977.

O'Neill, George, and Nena O'Neill. *Open Marriage*. New York: Evans, 1972.

Phelps, Susan, and Nancy Austin. *The Assertive Woman*. San Luis Obispo: Impact, 1975.

Powell, John. *Why Am I Afraid to Tell You Who I Am?* Niles, IL: Argus, 1969.

Rogers, Carl R. *Becoming Partners: Marriage and Its Alternatives*. New York: Delacorte, 1972. *Client Centered Therapy*. Boston: Houghton Mifflin, 1965.

Satir, Virginia. *Peoplemaking*. Palo Alto: Science and Behavior, 1972. *Your Many Faces*. Millbrae: Celestial Arts, 1978.

Sheehy, Gail. *Passages*. New York: Dutton, 1976.

Smith, Gerald Walker, and Alice I. Phillips. *Me, You and Us*. New York: Wyden, 1971.

Steiner, Claude. *Scripts People Live*. New York: Grove, 1974.

Weinstein, Grace W. *Children and Money: A Guide for Parents*. New York: David McKay, 1975.

Welsh, I. David, and Wanda Hughes. *Discipline*. New York: Hart, 1978.

Zilbergeld, Bernie. *Male Sexuality: A Guide to Sexual Fulfillment*. Boston: Little/Brown, 1978.

Index